Table of Contents

Introduction: Same-Sex and Opposite-Sex Couples: Exactly the Same?

Finally!

On June 26, 2013, the United States Supreme Court, in a ruling that had little to do with same-sex marriage, made it official: Same-sex couples are free to marry in California. It was long in coming and it followed a tortuous road, but the fight – at least in California – was finally over.

Few would have predicted this outcome, considering how the struggle began. In March, 2000, Californians flocked to the polls and by a 61% - 39% margin passed Proposition 22, which enacted Section 308.5 of the California Family Code. That statute, one of the shortest laws you will ever read, simply said: " Only marriage between a man and a woman is valid or recognized in California." But Proposition 22 was only a *statute*, and if a California statute conflicts with the California Constitution, the Constitution takes precedence. Of course, if a state statute conflicts with the United States Constitution (even if it does not conflict with a state constitution) the United States Constitution prevails.

That is how things stood on February 12, 2004, when Gavin Newsom, the newly-elected mayor of San Francisco, ordered his city clerk to begin issuing marriage licenses to same-sex couples, in direct contravention to

Proposition 22. His rationale was that Article I, Section 7 of the California Constitution, which guarantees to every California citizen the right to "equal protection" of the laws, gave him the right to do so. In other words, Mayor Newsom was declaring that Proposition 22 was unconstitutional.

The very next day, two organizations, the "Proposition 22 Legal Defense and Education Fund," and the "Campaign for California Families," sued to prohibit the San Francisco city clerk from issuing any more marriage licenses to same-sex couples.

Then things started to get really hot. On February 20, Governor Schwarzenegger ordered the state Attorney General, Bill Lockyer, to obtain "a definitive judicial resolution" of the issue. On March 14, in response to the suit brought by the two anti- same-sex marriage organizations, the California Supreme Court ordered that the issuance of marriage licenses to same-sex couples be stopped, pending a final resolution of the issue. The court also held that the 4,000 same-sex marriages that the San Francisco city clerk had performed under Mayor Newsom's order were void as being without judicial authority. It was these 4,000 marriages that formed the basis for the United States Supreme Court's decision nine years later.

The issue was decided by the California Supreme Court on May 15, 2008. In a case called *In re Marriage Cases*, the court ruled, by the narrowest of margins (a 4-3 decision) that Proposition 22 violated Article 1 Section 7 of the California Constitution. The majority opinion asserted that marriage is a "fundamental" right, and that any statute that denies one group a fundamental right based on their sexual orientation must be subject to "strict scrutiny," and that the opponents of same-sex marriage could not muster any argument that passed the "strict scrutiny" standard. The court said that its ruling would become effective in 30 days. On June 19, 2008, the court directed the California state government to begin performing same-sex marriages.

California was not the first state whose supreme court had ruled same-sex marriages unconstitutional. Massachusetts holds that honor. But the fight in California was far from over. On November 5, 2008, the voters in California, by a slim 52.2% - 47.7% majority, approved Proposition 8, a ballot initiative which amended the California Constitution by adding a provision that stated: "Only marriage between a man and a woman is valid or recognized in California." As Proposition 8 became part of the California Constitution, it could not violate the California Constitution, as Proposition 22 had. The issued remained, however, whether Proposition 8 violated the United States Constitution. Because it amended the California Constitution, Proposition 8 became effective immediately. Between June 19, 2008 and November 5, 2008, approximately 18,000 same-sex marriages had been performed in California. Those marriages remained valid. Everyone else was in limbo.

The validity of Proposition 8 was first appealed to the California Supreme Court, which ruled in 2009 in *Strauss v. Horton* that Proposition 8 did not violate the United States Constitution. It reasoned that Proposition 8 "carved out a limited exception to the state equal protection clause." Supreme Court Justice Carlos Moreno dissented, reasoning that the point of the Equal Protection Clause was to protect minority rights in the face of a majority bent on quashing those rights.

But the fight was far from over. The opponents of Proposition 8 challenged the constitutionality of Proposition 8 by bringing a suit in *federal* district court. In August, 2010, in *Perry v. Schwarzenegger*, Judge Vaughn Walker ruled that Proposition 8 violated both the Due Process Clause and the Equal Protection Clause of the United States Constitution, holding that there was no rational basis for Proposition 8's removal of the rights of a disfavored class. The proponents of Proposition 8 appealed Judge Walker's decision to the Ninth Circuit Court of Appeals, the federal appeals court that covers all of California and a number of other western states. The Ninth Circuit upheld Judge Walker's decision, holding that "Proposition 8 serves no purpose, and has no effect, other than to lessen the status and human dignity of gays and lesbians in California, and to officially reclassify their relationships and families as inferior to those of opposite-sex couples." The next – and last – stop could only be the United States Supreme Court.

And then something happened that only a lawyer could love. It is customary when someone challenges the validity of a state law in court that the state Attorney General will defend the law. After all, who is better positioned to defend a state law than the Attorney General, whose duty it is to defend the laws? But in this case, Governor Brown, acting through his Attorney General, refused to defend Proposition 8! If the Attorney General refused to defend Proposition 8 in court, who would? Who could?

A person may bring a lawsuit to challenge a law only if that person is directly affected by that law. For example, if the state enacts a tax law that Fred and Irving believe is unconstitutional, and Fred pays the tax and then argues its validity, Fred has *standing* to challenge the law. But if Irving has never paid the tax, and the state has never even suggested that Irving owes the tax, Irving cannot challenge the tax; he has no *standing*.

When Governor Brown refused to challenge the Ninth Circuit's decision in the United States Supreme Court, the people who originally fought to place Proposition 8 on the ballot took up the cause. But did they have standing, simply because they had brought a ballot initiative that ultimately proved successful, albeit narrowly? They argued that their opposition to same-sex marriage was not merely theoretical; that they had real "skin in the game" as a result of the work they had done putting the issue before the voters in the first place.

When the case (by then renamed *Hollingsworth v. Perry*) arrived at the Supreme Court, it was only secondarily a case involving same-sex marriage; it was primarily a "standing" case, because if the proponents had no standing, there was no one to challenge the lower court's decision. There is one thing the Supreme Court hates to do, which is to decide issues they don't need to decide.

The Supreme Court ruled that not only did the petitioners in *Hollingsworth v. Perry* have no standing to sue, but that the proponents of any ballot initiative *never* have standing to sue simply because they brought the initiative. So the Supreme Court never ruled on the issue of whether Proposition 8 violated the United States Constitution. That meant that the Ninth Circuit's ruling, which upheld Judge Walker's decision, was allowed to stand. Proposition 8 was unconstitutional, but only because there was no one who had standing to challenge it. Sometimes, that's how laws are made. No one ever promised it would be pretty.

Same Day: Another Big Decision

Hollingsworth v. Perry was not the only case the Supreme Court decided on June 26, 2013. *Hollingsworth* was significant only for California safe-sex couples, giving them the right to marry. But *United States v. Windsor* had – and will continue to have – far-reaching national significance. It may turn out to be the case that started the ball rolling that resulted in all laws prohibiting same-sex marriage being overturned.

In *Windsor*, the Supreme Court was called upon to decide the constitutionality of Section 3 of the federal Defense of Marriage Act, ("DOMA"). Section 3 provides that in any federal statute or rule, the word "marriage"

"…means only a legal union between one man and one woman

as husband and wife, and the word 'spouse'
refers only to a
person of the opposite sex who is a husband
or wife."

For example, if the Internal Revenue Code says that married couples can file a joint income tax return, it means that only opposite-sex couples can file such a return, not same-sex couples, even if that couple resides in a state the permits same-sex marriages and even if the couple was legally married in such a state. Bottom line: Any and all benefits that any federal law provides to married couples are denied to same-sex couples. How many statutes are there, similar to the tax code, that draw distinctions between married couples and single persons? Approximately 1,100!

United States v. Windsor arose in a tax context. In 2007, Edith Windsor and Thea Spyer were legally married in Canada, which recognizes same-sex marriages. Later, the couple moved to New York. In 2008, Governor David Patterson issued an executive order to the effect that New York State would recognize same-sex marriages performed in states (or foreign countries) that provide for such marriages. In 2009, Thea Spyer died. She left her entire estate to Edith Windsor. As we shall see in greater detail in Chapter 4, if a person leaves his or her estate to a surviving spouse, there are no estate taxes when the first spouse dies. If a single person dies, or if a married person leaves his or her estate to someone other than a surviving spouse, there may very well be an estate tax imposed when that person dies. And if the estate is large enough, the tax can be very steep. But since Thea Spyer left her entire estate to Edith Windsor, there should not have been an estate tax imposed on Thea Spyer's estate.

But that's when Section 3 of DOMA kicked in. By defining "marriage" for federal purposes as only the marriage of a man and a woman, Thea Spyer's estate did not qualify for the tax deferral granted to opposite-sex couples. The estate tax was $363,053, which Edith Windsor paid. She requested a refund, which was denied. The issue before the Supreme Court was whether Section 3 of DOMA was constitutional. Specifically, the issue was whether Section 3's blanket denial of all federal benefits to *legal* same-sex couples, i.e. same-sex couples married in jurisdictions that permit same-sex marriage, contravened the "equal protection" clause contained in the Fifth Amendment of the United States Constitution. Generally, if a statute draws a distinction between certain classes of citizens, such as same-sex and opposite-sex couples, there must be some "rational basis" for the distinction. A simple desire to discriminate against one group of citizens isn't enough.

The proponents of Section 3 of DOMA were hard-pressed to offer any rational explanation for denying federal benefits to same-sex couples that were already legally married.
In a 5-4 decision, the Supreme Court ruled that Section 3 of DOMA was an unconstitutional "deprivation of the liberty of the person protected by the Fifth Amendment." Edith Windsor got her tax refund.

It's important to note what *United States v. Windsor* does <u>not</u> say. It does not say that all federal statutes must treat same-sex and opposite-sex couples the same. It does not say that a state must permit same-sex marriages. It says only that if the voters in a state elect to allow same-sex marriages, DOMA's attempt to override that decision is unconstitutional. It is interesting, however, that in a ringing dissent, Justice Antonin Scalia predicted that the Court's ruling in *Windsor* was so close to ruling that all state statutes barring same-sex marriage are unconstitutional that the next case that arrived at the Supreme Court would result in such a conclusion. His prediction has proved to be accurate. Following *Windsor*, the federal appeals courts for the fourth circuit (which includes Virginia, Maryland, the Carolinas and West Virginia), the seventh circuit (which includes Illinois and Wisconsin) and the ninth and tenth circuits (the entire western half of the United States) have all ruled that state statutes barring same-sex marriage are unconstitutional, effectively legalizing same-sex marriage in every state within those circuits. Of course, the United States Supreme Court could overturn the decision of any federal appeals court. But on October 26, 2014, the Supreme Court declined the hear appeals from Indiana, Oklahoma, Virginia and Wisconsin.

As a result of *United States v. Windsor*, all distinctions contained in *federal* statutes and regulations between opposite-sex and same-sex marriages are abolished. Any federal benefit conferred on opposite-sex couples is now conferred on an equal basis on same-sex couples, provided, of course, that the same-sex couple was married in one of the 36 states and the District of Columbia that, as of this writing, permit same-sex marriage.

But it doesn't end there. After the decision in *Windsor*, Attorney General Eric Holder announced that the federal government would treat same-sex couples on the same basis as opposite-sex couples, even if the couple relocates from the state in which they were married to a state that does not recognize same-sex marriage.

Exactly the Same?

Do same-sex couples now stand on an equal footing with opposite-sex couples? Not exactly. *United States v. Windsor* struck down Section 3 of DOMA. It left standing Section 2, which provides that no state shall be required to give effect to any statute of another state…

"…respecting a relationship between persons of the same sex that is

treated as a marriage under the laws of such other State…or right or

claim arising out of such relationship."

In other words, if one state allows same-sex marriage, another state is not required to honor a marriage performed in that state. Section 2 seems to directly contradict Article IV Section 1 of the United States Constitution, the so-called "Full Faith and Credit Clause," which provides, in part:

"Full faith and credit shall be given in each state to the public

acts, records, and judicial proceedings of every other state."

Over the years, the Supreme Court has drawn a distinction between the *judgments* that the courts of one state render – which another state must honor under the Full Faith and Credit Clause – and the *laws* of one state, which another state does not necessarily need to honor in all circumstances. Whether Section 2's blanket exemption of same-sex marriage laws from the purview of the Full Faith and Credit Clause is constitutional remains to be seen.

The Supreme Court in *Windsor* did not rule on Section 2 because it wasn't asked to.

But the law, as it stands today, is that same-sex and opposite-sex couples are equal for all *federal* law purposes, but not for state law purposes. That can place same-sex couples in some weird situations. For example, if a same-sex couple is married in California, and then moves to Louisiana, (a state that as of today does not recognize same-sex marriage) the couple not only may, but must file their income tax return as if they are married, either as married filing jointly or married filing separately. But they may not file their Louisiana state income tax return as a married couple because they are not deemed to be married in Louisiana. Whatever distinctions Louisiana draws between married couples and single persons applies to same-sex couples in Louisiana, which continues to treat the same-sex married couple as legal strangers.

As of this writing, the fight is close to coming to a dramatic conclusion, one way or another. On January 16, 2015, the Supreme Court decided to hear four cases from Ohio, Kentucky, Tennessee and Michigan. In one of those cases, the Supreme Court will decide whether Section 2 of DOMA is constitutional. In the other cases, the Supreme Court will decide the basic question, i.e. whether a state statute prohibiting same-sex marriage violates the Equal Protection Clause of the United States Constitution. If the Supreme Court rules that a state cannot prohibit same-sex marriage, the DOMA issue becomes irrelevant. Arguments will be heard in April, with decisions expected by the end of the Supreme Court's term in June. By the time you read these pages, we will probably know whether the right of same-sex couples to marry is mandated by the United States Constitution.

If a majority of the nine justices strike down all state laws prohibiting same-sex marriage, there will be a delicious irony in it, in that Justice Antonin Scalia, the most consistent and vociferous opponent of same-sex marriage, will have predicted it. In 2003, in *Lawrence v. Texas*, the Supreme Court struck down a Texas law outlawing "sodomy." In Justice Kennedy's majority opinion, he wrote that the Constitution protects "adult persons in deciding how to conduct their private lives in matters pertaining to sex." But he also took pains to point out that this decision was not meant to imply that this reasoning did not apply to same-sex marriage. Not so fast, wrote Justice Scalia in another ringing dissent. If a state cannot ban homosexual sex "what justification could there possibly be for denying the benefits of marriage to homosexual couples exercising the liberty protected by the Constitution?" What justification, indeed?

If all state statutes banning same-sex marriage are struck down, will same-sex and opposite-sex couples be the same? Not really. In one practical sense, they are very different. Opposite-sex couples generally marry when they please to. On rare occasion a very young couple must wait until they are old enough to marry, or obtain parental consent. In most cases, they start out with nothing, and build up their assets as they go through life. But that's not the case with many same-sex couples, many who have had to wait years – or decades – to be able to marry. Having waited, they are older, and likely will have acquired substantial assets prior to the marriage. Many of them have been in prior *opposite-sex* marriages, often with children. These couples have very different financial, tax, and estate planning goals than do young opposite-sex couples just starting out in life.

Same-sex couples also have an option in California that heterosexuals, whose only choice is to marry or remain single, do not have. Before California same-sex couples obtained the unqualified right to marry by virtue of *United States v. Windsor*, they had the option to enter into *registered domestic partnerships*. As we shall see later, couples who were registered domestic partners obtained all of the benefits (and detriments) of married couples under California law, but none of the benefits and detriments conferred upon married couples under *federal* law. That is still the case for registered domestic partners, even after *United States v. Windsor*. In a number of states that had provided for civil unions prior to the advent of same-sex marriage, the statutes providing for civil unions were later subsumed into the statutes providing for same-sex marriage. But not California. Same-sex couples still enjoy the option of marriage or registering as domestic partners. It is likely that, with every passing year, the number of same-sex couples electing not to marry but instead electing to register as domestic partners will decline. But, as we shall also see, there may be some same-sex couples who will realize that the tax and other detriments of marriage outweigh the benefits and who will elect to remain registered domestic partners or who will register as such in the first instance.

Chapter 1
The Basics: Separate Property and Community Property

And further more just from stalling and stalling and stalling
the wedding trip,
a person can develop La grippe.
And when they get on the train to Niagra, she can hear the
church bells chime.
The compartment is air conditioned and the mood sublime.
Then they get off at Saratoga for the fourteenth time,
A person can develop La Grippe, La Grippe, La post-nasal
drip,
With the wheezes, and the sneezes, and the sinuses really
a pip!
From a lack of community property and a feeling she's
getting too old,
A person can develop a big, bad cold!
-- "Adelaide's Lament" from "Guys and
Dolls"

In "Guys and Dolls," Adelaide has been Nathan
Detroit's girlfriend for close to two decades. Nathan
Detroit keeps promising marriage, but keeps putting it off.
One of Adelaide's "laments" is a lack of community
property. It's a great lyric, but contains a considerable
amount of poetic license. All of "Guys and Dolls" takes
place within walking distance of Times Square in New
York City. As there are only ten states that have
community property,[1] not including New York, even if

---

[1] Arizona, Idaho, Louisiana, Nevada, New Mexico, Texas, Washington,
Wisconsin and, of course, California. Alaska permits spouses to opt
into community property by contract.

Nathan Detroit pops the question – as he does at the end of the play – Adelaide, unless she and Nathan Detroit relocate elsewhere – will always suffer from a lack of community property.

Prior to same-sex marriage becoming legal in California, same-sex couples did not need to worry about the distinctions between separate and community property.[2] Now they do.

What is Separate (and Community) Property?

Whether the property of a married couple is "separate" or "community" is extremely important, with far-ranging consequences. We'll discuss the consequences of separate and community property later in this chapter. But first, it's important to understand just what separate and community property is. Brace yourself. This is one area where common sense isn't a guide and looks can be deceiving.

If a person in California is not married, all of the person's property is "separate;" It belongs only to him or her. If the property has a title – such as real estate – and the person's name is on the title, it means that the person on the title is the owner. If property is a person's separate property, only that person has the right to sell, trade, lease or otherwise deal with the property. The fact that a bank may have a mortgage on the property doesn't change this fact. The bank has a security interest in the property and is entitled to part of the sales proceeds if the property is sold,

---

[2] California Registered Domestic Partners do fall within the California community property law, discussed later in this chapter.

but it doesn't change the fact that the person on the title is the sole owner of the property.

But if two people in California marry (or become Registered Domestic Partners), things become more complicated. A married couple's property can be separate or community property. Some of the assets may be separate, some may be community, and the nature of an asset as separate or community can change during the course of the marriage, without the married couple even being aware of it.

But what is community property? Sadly, California law does not provide us with a very good definition. Generally, if property is acquired by a married couple during the marriage, the property is not owned by either spouse, but by the *community estate*, and each spouse owns a one-half interest in the community estate. California law also says that if there is any doubt about whether an asset is the separate property of either spouse or is community property, you can presume that it's community property. Not only is property of any kind (with a couple of minor exceptions) that is acquired during the marriage community property, but the *earnings* of either spouse earned during the marriage are also community property.

The key to understanding California community property is to remember one thing: After people marry, *titles don't control*! Here is an example that proves the point. Jane Smith and June Smith are married in California. Jane works in a lumber yard. Every two weeks, Jane receives a paycheck for $1,000. The paycheck is made payable to "Jane Smith." Of the $1,000, Jane Smith owns $500, and June Smith owns $500. That's because Jane Smith's wages, earned during the marriage, are community property. Each owns half.

Here's another example: Edward Ennis and Irving Ennis are married. They buy a home costing $400,000 in Lancaster. Each withdraws $20,000 from his checking account (with funds deposited from each of their earnings during the marriage), and they each co-sign a $360,000 note. Irving is having difficulties with creditors, so they decide to put only Edward's name on the deed. The home is community property. The name on the deed doesn't control. But let's assume that Irving buys a parcel of real estate with funds that he inherited, and he puts his and Edward's name on the title. There is a *presumption* of community property, one that, in this case, Irving might be able to overcome to prove that the property is really his separate property.

There isn't a divorce lawyer in California who at some point hasn't had a client say to him or her: "Don't worry about that piece of property in the divorce. Only my name is on it." Right. That's when the divorce lawyer has to impart the bad news. Between married couples, titles to property don't decide the issue. We need to look further to determine if the property is separate, community, or a combination of each.

But to complicate matters much further, not all of the property in California that is owned by married couples is community property. There are some big exceptions, as follows:

• *Property that was owned prior to the marriage retains its character as separate property during the marriage.* This is the biggest exception. As a general rule, you don't lose anything by getting married in California. As we have seen, if you owned an asset when you were a single person, it had to be your separate property. On the day after the wedding, and for every day of the marriage thereafter, that asset remains your separate property. However, as we shall see shortly, that asset can become community property if you *commingle* it with community property.

• *The appreciation on California separate property during the marriage remains separate property.* Let's assume you own a condo that has a market value of $400,000 on the day you're married. Nine years later, you're still married, and the condo is now worth $700,000. The whole $700,000 is still your separate property, the same as it would have been had you never married. Once again, this result changes if there has been a commingling of separate and community property.

• *All property acquired after marriage by "gift, bequest, devise or descent."*[3] The words "bequest, devise or descent" is lawyerspeak for property received from a dead person. So if you inherit property during the marriage, or someone makes you a gift of property during the marriage, the property is your separate property. If it appreciates in value during the marriage, the appreciation is also your separate property.

• *The rents and profits from separate property is separate property.* Let's assume you own an apartment building that is your separate property. After collecting all of the rent and deducting all of the expenses from the operations of the building, you turn a profit on the building during the year. The profit is your separate property.

---

[3] Family Code §770(a)(2).

There are a few minor areas where community property (or separate property) is created or affected by statute (not so minor if it affects you), as follows:

• *An educational degree or professional license can be a community asset.* Let's assume that Mandy and Sandy are married in California. Shortly after they marry, Mandy decides to go to law school. Sandy works as a bartender. Mandy takes out a student loan to pay for the tuition, books and fees. Sandy supports them both while Mandy is studying. The little savings that Mandy and Sandy had before they married is depleted as a result of Mandy not working for three years. Shortly after Mandy graduates from law school, they begin paying off Mandy's student loan with Sandy's earnings as a bartender.

Shortly after that, Mandy files a petition seeking a divorce. They really don't have any assets to divide, having spent it all for law school. When it comes to paying *spousal support* (a/k/a "alimony"), if anything, Sandy should pay maintenance to Mandy, because Sandy had an income during the marriage; Mandy did not.

There is, of course, the matter of that law degree that Mandy picked up during the marriage, a law degree that was paid for in part with Sandy's earnings, which was, of course community property, and which was facilitated by the student loan that was repaid, in part, with Sandy's earnings. Should the law degree not count for something in the divorce?

The California Family Code thinks so, and it contains a special provision for all of the Mandys and Sandys of California. Section 2641 of the Family Code provides that, in a divorce, the one spouse who obtained "education or training" during the marriage that

21

"substantially enhances" that spouse's earning capacity is required to reimburse the community for the contributions that the community made in pursuing that education and training. The reimbursement bears legal interest, measured from the time that the contribution was made. In other words, one half of the amounts Sandy took out of her paycheck – plus interest – is a credit to Sandy when Sandy and Mandy get divorced. She gets a credit for whatever she spent towards Mandy's law degree, even if she took the money out of her paycheck *before* Sandy and Many were married.

But let's change the facts. Shortly after graduating from law school, Mandy lands a job at Huge & Enormous, LLP, an international law firm. In time, she earns a seven figure annual income, allowing Sandy to quit her job as a bartender. They travel all over the world, and acquire residences in Palm Beach, Maui and Majorca. Twenty-five years after Mandy's graduation from law school, Mandy files a divorce petition. Is Sandy still entitled to a credit for the amounts that she spent towards Mandy's law degree 28 years ago? It seems that after all this time, Sandy has benefitted from Mandy's law degree as much as Mandy has. Section 2641 thinks so. It provides that the amount that Sandy is entitled to receive is reduced to the extent that the community has benefitted from Mandy's enhanced earning capacity. It also provides a *rebuttable presumption* that if the marriage lasted more than ten years, the community has benefitted from the law degree, reducing (perhaps to zero) the amount of reimbursement to the community. But if the marriage lasted less than ten years, the rebuttable presumption is that the community was not benefitted from the enhanced education, requiring reimbursement. A rebuttable presumption is just that. Sandy can try to prove that the community was not benefitted from Mandy's law degree, which will be an uphill fight in light of the homes in Palm Beach, Maui and Majorca.

• *Whether an award for personal injuries is community property or separate property depends upon when the cause of action arose.*

Fred and Ned, who are living together in San Diego, decide to get married. While driving to his tailor to be fitted for his tuxedo, Fred is rear-ended by a drunk driver. Fred suffers substantial injuries, incurs considerable hospital bills, and misses work for two weeks. After Fred is released from the hospital, Fred files a lawsuit against the drunk driver. Fred and Ned then get married in 2014. The trial is set for 2015. On the morning of the trial, Fred's lawyer and the lawyer for the drunk driver's insurance carrier settle the case for $500,000. Fred receives a check the next week. Is the $500,000 Fred's separate property, or is it community property? Section 780 of the California Family Code provides the answer. Because the cause of action (the accident) arose before Fred and Ned were married, the $500,000 is Fred's separate property. As usual, there is an exception. If Ned was required to dig into his pocket as a result of Fred's injuries, for example, to pay for the ambulance and Fred's physical therapy, Ned is entitled to a contribution.

Once again, let's change the facts. On the day after the wedding, Fred is rear-ended by a drunk driver while returning his tuxedo to his tailor. In other words, the cause of action arose during the marriage. Clearly, when the insurance company's check arrives, the settlement proceeds are community property. But let's assume that after the accident but before the settlement proceeds arrive, Fred and Ned separate. In that case, the settlement proceeds are Fred's separate property, even if their separation has not been formalized by a court-approved settlement agreement.[4]

We saw that wages earned during the marriage are community property. There's an exception to that general rule. Once the spouses are *legally separated*, there really is no longer a community estate, and everything thereafter is separate, as fully as if the spouses were finally divorced. For this rule, moving out and spending a few nights on your buddy's couch while things cool off doesn't qualify. For the community estate to end, there must be a judgment of legal separation, in writing and blessed by a judge.

Property that is acquired by California spouses while domiciled in California is community property, even if the property is located in a state that does not recognize community property.[5]

But things get much more complicated if property is acquired by spouses while domiciled in another state that does not recognize community property. Let's assume Bill and Roy are married in New York State, a state that does not have community property. While residing in New York, they acquire an investment property. They then move to California. After living in California for a few years, they decide to divorce. The New York investment property is something called *quasi-community property*. As a general rule, the divorce court will divide the property as if it were community property.

Things can get still more complicated. We said that the earnings of a spouse are community property. Let's assume that Susan and Janet are married in California.

---

[4] Family Code §782(a)(2).
[5] Family Code §760.

Janet runs a successful accounting practice. If Janet withdraws her earnings from the accounting practice during the marriage, clearly those earnings are community property. But let's assume that on the day that Janet and Susan are divorced, Janet's accounting practice had $1 million in accounts receivable. Most of the money was earned during the marriage, but not received until after the marriage ceased. Generally, the accounts receivable are community property. But let's assume that Janet had been engaged to perform an audit for a corporate client. She completed part of the work during the marriage, but finished the audit only after the divorce was final. It is likely that the divorce court will allocate the accounts receivable, part as community property and part as Janet's separate property. If you haven't guessed it already, this is the kind of stuff that makes divorce lawyers rich.

This example reveals yet another complicating factor: Not only can property be community property, but so can a spouse's *time and efforts*. Let's assume that Don and Fred are married. Don is an amateur sculptor, and spends every weekend in his studio. He sells his stuff at art fairs. The money he earns is community property. That's an obvious example. Here's one that is less so. When Don and Fred were married, Fred had a substantial stock portfolio. Clearly, the stock portfolio is separate property. We have also seen that the appreciation in the portfolio during the marriage is also Fred's separate property. But Fred spends a considerable amount of time every week reading analysts reports, attending shareholders' meetings, and consulting with financial planners. When Don and Fred divorce, is part of the stock portfolio community property? Yes, it is. How much is community property? Hard to say. This is where divorce lawyers get *really* rich.

Let's assume that one – but only one – of two spouses is involved in a car accident, and sues the other driver. The case goes to trial, and the one spouse is awarded $1 million in damages. Is the $1 million community property or separate property? It depends. If the accident occurred while the spouses were married and the award is received during the marriage, the award is community property. But if the accident occurred before the spouses were married but was received after the spouses were married, the award is the separate property of the injured spouse. If the accident occurred after the marriage but while the spouses are separated, the award is the separate property of the injured spouse.[6]

As we shall see shortly, it's possible – and easy – to completely override the law and avoid all of this complexity by entering into a pre-marital agreement or a post-marital agreement that sets forth what is, and is not, community property and separate property.

Commingling of Separate and Community Property

It is here that things get really complicated. It's very possible for a parcel of property to start out its life during a marriage as one spouse's separate property, but be changed ("transmuted," in the legalese) into community property if it's commingled with community property. As we shall see shortly, commingling of separate and community property is a lot easier than you might think it is. In fact, commingling is difficult to avoid.

---

[6] Family Code §781.

Let's take an obvious example. Donna and Deanna have been married a very long time. Prior to their marriage, they each had a separate checking account. When they married, they opened a joint checking account, and emptied their separate checking accounts into the joint account. They deposited their paychecks into the account, and made withdrawals from the account. When they decided to divorce, there was $50,000 in the joint checking account. It's been years since they first opened the joint account, and they have no idea what happened to the original deposits into the account. It's safe to say that since neither of them can trace the money in the account to the original separate property, the entire $50,000 is community property, and each will get half in the divorce.

Contrary to popular belief, it isn't the act of depositing the separate property into the joint account that results in the commingling. If either Donna and Deanna were able to trace each of their original deposits into the joint account, it might be possible for one of them to prove that the joint account should not be divided equally. It's the inability to trace the current funds to the original separate property that results in the current funds being presumed to be community property, a presumption that neither of them can overcome.

Donna and Deanna's joint checking account is an obvious example of commingling. Now let's assume that at the time Donna and Deanna married, Donna owned a residence in Los Angeles that was worth $400,000. There was a $100,000 balance due on the mortgage, resulting in $300,000 in equity. Clearly, the residence is Donna's separate property, and any appreciation in the residence during her marriage to Deanna is also her separate property. Donna is a pediatrician. Every month, she draws a paycheck from her medical practice. She takes part of her paycheck and pays the mortgage. Twice a year, she takes part of her paycheck and pays the property taxes. As we have seen, Donna's income is community property, which means that half of Donna's income belongs to Deanna. Every month, when Donna paid the mortgage, she used part of Deanna's community property to service her separate property. Ditto when Donna paid the property taxes. The new deck? The solar panels? The landscaping? Ditto, ditto, ditto.

Let's assume that by the time Donna and Deanna file for divorce, Donna has taken $47,234 of Deanna's share of the community property to service her separate property. The residence has appreciated to $900,000. Is Deanna entitled to reimbursement of $47,234 for the contributions she made to Donna's property? It would seem (and it is) that Deanna is entitled to lots more than a dollar-for-dollar reimbursement of the community property she contributed to Donna's property. After all, her contributions helped to residence appreciate in value. If Donna and Deanna have been married long enough, it's possible that Deanna has a 50% interest in the residence.

It's possible for separate property to be transmuted to community property even if no compensation is contributed to service a spouse's separate property. Let's assume that Dave and Al are married. Shortly before the marriage, Dave founded a corporation that develops software. He obtained a stock certificate for 100 shares that represents a 50% ownership interest in the corporation. His friend Chris owns the other 50%. Clearly, the shares of stock are Dave's separate property. We have seen that the appreciation in separate property during the marriage is also separate property. After Dave marries Al, he works nights and weekends developing the software and bringing it to market. Both Dave and Chris decide they cannot take a salary, and plow whatever revenues there are into software development. When Dave and Al separate, the business still hasn't turned a profit, Dave hasn't drawn a salary, but Dave's shares have appreciated from nothing to $1 million. Is it all Dave's separate property? Hardly. As we have seen, Dave's time and efforts are also a community asset which Dave contributed to service his separate asset. Part of the appreciation in Dave's stock is Al's community property which he has a right to receive in the divorce. How much of the appreciation is Al's? It's very difficult to say, and this is what makes divorce lawyers (and many forensic accountants) very, very rich.

Once again, this result is easily avoidable, with a pre-marital or a post-marital agreement.

Community Property v. Separate Property: Why does it Matter?

Ascertaining whether a married couple's assets are community property or separate property, or which are community and which are separate, is not the end of the inquiry. It's only the beginning. Whether property is community or separate is important in four distinct areas, as follows:

- *Who gets what assets in a divorce?*

- *Which assets may a spouse give away, either during lifetime or at death?*

- *Which assets may be attached or seized in payment of the debts of a spouse?*

• *Which assets may be controlled by a spouse during the marriage?*

For many married couples, the issue of whether assets are community or separate property never arises. If the couple remains married throughout their joint lifetimes, are never subject to a lawsuit, and if the first spouse to die leaves everything to the surviving spouse, it never mattered whether a particular asset – or any of the assets – was community or separate property. But life is often not that happy, or simple. Let's look at each separately.

Who gets what assets in a divorce?

We've already examined this area in some depth. As a general rule, if the parties cannot agree between themselves, a divorce court judge is required to divide the community property equally, awarding half to each spouse. Also as a general rule, the divorce court judge will award all of the separate property to that spouse or to those spouses who can prove that a particular asset is their separate property, either because the asset was owned by the spouse prior to the marriage or was received by the spouse by means of a gift or by inheritance, and was never commingled or transmuted into community property.

There are some exceptions to the general rule (do you detect a pattern here?). If the divorce court judge determines that one spouse has *dissipated* the community property, the judge may dock that spouse, requiring that the spouse make a reimbursement to the community. Here's an example: Joe and Jimmy are married. Jimmy receives a divorce petition from Joe, who has just moved out of the house. In a fit of anger, Jimmy removes the entire $100,000 from their joint checking account, flies to Las

Vegas, buys $100,000 in chips, strides up to the roulette table, places all the chips on double zero and blows it all. One might conclude that Jimmy has dissipated community funds, and that divorce court judge will hold Jimmy to account. But Jimmy's not done. After his spree at the roulette table, Jimmy finds the most expensive haberdasher in Las Vegas, and runs up a $10,000 balance on his credit card. The divorce court judge will likely find that that $10,000 debt is not a community debt, but a separate debt, ordering Jimmy to pay it. It's important to note that if the credit card were in both Joe's name and Jimmy's name, the fact that the divorce court judge ordered only Jimmy to pay does not relieve Joe of the debt. The bank could sue Joe, as well as Jimmy, on the debt.

In most cases, the requirement that community property be divided equally results in a fair result. It is, in fact, the rationale for having community property. But California's community property law can result in severe injustice, something that is often avoided in states that do not have a community property law. Here's how.

Let's assume that Earl and Maria were married in California in 1970. At the time of the marriage, Earl owned a few acres of orange groves in Irvine and a few shares of stock in the Los Angeles Times Company, which he was awarded as a linotypist. Maria owned nothing. When Irvine began to grow around the orange groves, the property became more and more valuable. Finally, Earl felt he couldn't hold out any longer, and in 1989 sold the land for $20 million. An upscale mall and a concert hall now sit on what were once his orange trees. The Los Angeles Times stock split 50 to 1, and was worth $9 million when Earl sold it. Earl took the proceeds from the sale of the property and the sale of the stock and bought California municipal bonds. In 2010, after 40 years of marriage, Earl sued Maria for divorce. Earl might have to pay Maria a substantial amount in spousal support, but as far as the assets are concerned, Maria gets nothing. Having owned the property prior to marriage, both the original assets, and all of the appreciation on those assets, and all of the proceeds from the sale of the assets, are still Earl's separate property. Maria might be able to prove that Earl expended some of his time and energies on the properties, but it does not appear likely.

That is not the result in most states that do not have community property, i.e. in *separate property* states. In those states, when a couple divorces, all of the property of both spouses suddenly becomes *marital property*, and is divided according to a laundry list of factors, including the length of the marriage, the life style each of the spouses has become accustomed to, the ability of each spouse to earn income following the divorce, and the judge's mood on the day of the hearing. But nobody gets stuck with nothing, which is a possible result in California.

• All About Qualified Domestic Relations Orders.

It is often the case that one (or both) spouses contributed to a 401(k) plan or pension plan during the marriage. It's also possible that the spouse's employer matched the contributions that the divorcing spouse made. As we have seen, the wages and salaries that a spouse receives during the marriage is community property. Should not the contributions that an employee or the employee's employer made to the 401(k) plan or pension plan also be community property? Yes, they are.

But there's a problem. Most employer-sponsored 401(k) plans, pension plans, profit-sharing plans and "defined benefit" plans are "qualified" plans under the

Employee Retirement Income Security Act of 1974 ("ERISA"). There are many things that a retirement plan must include in order to be a "qualified plan," and one of them is an "anti-alienation" clause, which must state that nobody – absolutely nobody – can get at an employee's plan account other than the employee. You don't believe it? Let's assume that Johnny gets dead drunk one night, manages to open and start his car, and traveling on the wrong side of the freeway rams a school bus full of girl scouts, killing ten. He is charged and convicted of vehicular homicide. The judge orders Johnny to pay $10 million in restitution to the families of the victims. Can the District Attorney access Johnny's 401(k) plan to pay the restitution award? Not a chance. Let's assume that Johnny makes a contribution to his 401(k) after he's arrested, assuming that he will get stuck with a restitution award. Can the District Attorney access the money contributed after the accident? Not a chance. The anti-alienation provision of every ERISA qualified plan means that no one, ever, under any circumstances can access an employee's account except the employee.

With one exception. The ERISA statute contains a special provision that permits a divorcing spouse to gain access to the other spouse's qualified plan assets. If the divorce court judge determines that a part of a spouse's qualified plan consists of the other spouse's community property, the judge can issue a *qualified domestic relations order,* or "QDRO." It is an order directed at the administrator of the qualified plan, ordering the administrator to distribute plan assets to someone other than the plan participant. That "someone" can only be a spouse, a former spouse, a dependent child or other dependent. If the parties to a divorce enter into a settlement agreement between themselves, that's not enough to force the plan administrator to part with the funds; a judge must order the administrator to release them.

The ability of a divorcing spouse to obtain a distribution of plan assets is not unlimited. Generally, the divorcing spouse doesn't have any rights to the plan assets that are superior to the rights of his or her spouse. For example, if the plan provides that an employee cannot receive plan distributions until retirement at age 62, then the employee's spouse cannot obtain a QDRO ordering the plan administrator to make a distribution before the employee turns 62. If, however, the plan permits the employee to take distributions at age 58, but the employee has elected not to take them until age 62, then the employee's spouse will be able to obtain a QDRO ordering distributions to the spouse at the earlier time.

Which assets may a spouse give away, either during lifetime or at death?

If you're married, what you can give away is a function of whether your property is community property or separate property. You have probably guessed by now that if you own separate property, you can write a Will or a trust (more on that in Chapter 4) and give your separate property to whomever you wish. But since you own only half of the community property, you can give away only half of the community property in your Will or by means of a trust. Similarly, you can make a valid gift of all of your separate property but only half of the community property during your lifetime. If a married person in California decides one day to empty out the joint bank account and give it to his Uncle Ned, and the gift is followed by a divorce, the spouse who withdrew the bank account will no doubt be required to reimburse the community to the extent of one-half of the cash that went to Uncle Ned.

Just as we saw with respect to Earl and Maria in the case of a divorce, the operation of the California community property law has the potential for real injustice. Let's assume that Earl and Maria remained married, but after 40 years of marriage to Maria, Earl died. As in our prior example, Earl's separate property was worth $29 million at the time of his death. There is no community property. Let's also assume that a month before Earl died, he met and became infatuated with a waitress at a roadhouse. So he had his lawyer draw up a Will leaving everything to the waitress. Maria got nothing. The Will was properly drafted and witnessed. Earl may have been terribly foolish, but he was not insane. Does the waitress get everything and Maria nothing? Unless Maria can somehow invalidate the Will by proving that Earl was *non compos mentis*, i.e., not of sound mind, or that someone had a gun pointed at Earl's head when he wrote the Will, it's likely that the Will is valid, and that Maria gets nothing.

Just as an aside, it's interesting to note that in most states that do not have community property, it's not possible to do what Earl did, viz., disinherit a spouse. Most non-community property states give a surviving spouse a *right of election*, which gives the surviving spouse the right to take either whatever the spouse was left in the Will or trust, or whatever the state statute provides. Most state statutes give the surviving spouse the right to take either 30%, a third or as much as half of whatever his or her spouse owned, even if it was all the separate property of the deceased spouse. Some state right-of-election laws make the amount of the election a function of whether there are also surviving children, but many do not. In no state with a spousal right of election could Earl do what he did to Maria: leave her with nothing.

• *Community property, separate property and intestacy*

Let's assume that Earl intended to write a Will leaving everything to the waitress at the roadhouse, but he never quite got around to writing it. He had no other Will or trust. That means that Earl died *intestate*, i.e. without a Will.

Who gets Earl's $29 million estate? That depends. If the assets were community property, then Earl's surviving spouse gets one-half of the community property.[7] Why only one-half? Because the surviving spouse already owned the other half, so that only the other half passes to the surviving spouse.

But let's assume, as we have before, that all of Earl's $29 million was his separate property. Who gets it? If Earl and Maria had one child, then Maria gets half of Earl's estate, and the child gets the other half. If Maria and Earl had two or more children, then Maria gets a third of Earl's estate, and the children divide the remaining two-thirds among themselves, equally. If Earl and Maria had no children, and Earl had no surviving parents or siblings and if there are no children of any of Earl's predeceased siblings, then, and only then, will Maria inherit all of Earl's separate property.[8] Needless to say, if Maria realizes during her marriage to Earl that all or a substantial portion of Earl's estate is separate property, it is important for

---

[7] Probate Code §6401(a).
[8] Probate Code §6401(c).

Maria to assure that Earl (a) writes a Will and (b) stays out of roadhouses.[9]

Which assets may be attached or seized in payment of the debts of a spouse?

The issue of which of a married couple's assets may be seized by a third party creditor is probably the most misunderstood and overlooked difference between separate property and community property. On many occasions, this is the issue that determines whether couples elect to marry or elect to remain unmarried. It is often the determining factor as to whether a couple will enter into a premarital ("pre-nuptial") agreement if they are not yet married or whether they enter into a post-nuptial agreement after marriage (more on that in Chapter 2). On some occasions, the hot breath of a creditor may even result in a married couple getting a divorce. Bottom line: Which creditors can get at what assets when a couple is married is a very big issue.

• *The General Rules*

The most important statute you will read about in this book is §910 of the California Family Code. It's worth reading in full:

"(a) Except as otherwise expressly provided by statute,
the community estate is liable for a debt incurred by either

---

[9] It has been estimated that approximately 90% of all lawsuits contesting the validity of a Will or trust involve the children of a first marriage against the second spouse of the deceased.

spouse *before or during* marriage, regardless of which spouse

has the management and control of the property and regardless

of whether one or both spouses are parties to the debt or to a

judgment for the debt." [Italics added.]

(b) 'During marriage' for purposes of this section does not

include the period during which the spouses are living separate and

apart before a judgment of dissolution of marriage or legal

separation of the parties."

We saw earlier in this chapter that if spouses own community property, each spouse owns an interest in half of the community property. If the spouses divorce, each spouse gets half of the community property. If a spouse dies, that spouse can leave only half of the community property in a Will or a trust; he or she doesn't own the other half. But if only one spouse incurs a debt, that spouse's creditor can access both halves of the community property, even if the other spouse did not join in the debt or isn't even aware of the debt.

Earlier in this chapter we visited Jane Smith, who works in a lumber yard and is married to June Smith. Once night, June Smith after having a few too many drinks a t the local bar, manages to get her car started but doesn't manage to get home before ramming Rev. Jones, a pedestrian. Rev. Jones brings a lawsuit only against June, and obtains a judgment against June. One day, *Jane* notices that her paycheck is a little short. That's when she learns that her paycheck has been *garnished* by Rev. Jones.

Is that possible? Can they take one spouse's wages to satisfy the debts of the other spouse? Absolutely. Jane Smith's paycheck is community property, and as such all of the community property can stand to answer for the debts of either spouse.[10]

And it gets worse. Let's assume that June Smith killed a pedestrian before Jane and June were married. After Jane and June are married, they pool their savings to make the down payment on a home. They make mortgage payments from their wages, and twice each year pay the property taxes with their joint savings. The home is titled in both of their names. Clearly, the home is community property. When the pedestrian sues June Smith for the injuries she caused prior to the marriage, can the pedestrian obtain a judgment and force the sale of the home in order to satisfy the judgment? Absolutely.

And it may get still worse. Let's assume that Jane Smith bought a home prior to her marriage to June. As we have seen, the home – and all the appreciation in the home – remains Jane's separate property. However, as we have also seen, it's not too difficult to transmute separate property into community property, even unwittingly. If, during the marriage, Jane and June use part of June's income to pay the mortgage and the property taxes, June builds up a community property interest in Jane's separate property, a community property interest that one of June's creditors can attach. In an extreme case, it could result in Jane losing her home.[11]

---

[10] All of the community property is subject to the debts of either spouse, but not all of Jane Smith's earnings are subject to garnishment. As a general rule in California, a creditor cannot take more than 25% of the "disposable" earnings during any pay period.

[11] For the purposes of this rule, "quasi-community property." i.e. property of a California married couple acquired   in a non-

This may be a good place to dispel the myth of the "homestead" exemption. Many Californians are under the sad misimpression that a creditor cannot take their residence because of the homestead exemption. If you're married in California (or in a registered domestic partnership) your homestead exemption is all of $100,000; $175,000 if you're over age 65 or disabled. That means that if your home is worth $1,000,000 and you owe $200,000 on it, your equity is $800,000. Someone wishing to acquire your home in a foreclosure sale might have to pay you $100,000 (or $175,000, as the case may be) but it wouldn't prevent the foreclosure. If your equity in the residence is only $100,000, it would prevent a foreclosure. So much for the homestead exemption.

The harsh rule of §910 is somewhat mitigated by §911 of the Family Code, which provides that the earnings of a married person are not subject to the *premarital* debts of the other spouse. That means that a creditor of a debtor-spouse cannot garnish the wages of the other spouse for a debt that arose prior to the marriage. But once the earnings are paid out, those earnings are shielded from the other spouse's pre-marital debts only if the wage-earner spouse keeps the earnings in a segregated bank account to which the debtor-spouse has no access.

It's interesting how much easier life is in one of the forty states that do not have community property. In these states, if an asset is titled in the name of one spouse, that spouse owns it, and the creditors of the other spouse cannot get at it. The only exception in these states is if an asset is titled in the name of one spouse as a result of a

---

community property state, is treated the same as community property. Family Code §912.

fraudulent conveyance. Here's how that works: Let's assume that Bill and Carl are married in New York, a state that recognizes same-sex marriage but does not have community property. While married to Carl, Bill personally guaranteed a corporate debt, and it looks like the corporation will not be able to pay. Bill owns a vacation home in Saratoga Springs that is worth $1 million. He fears he might lose the vacation home if he is sued on his guaranty. So he transfers the title to the vacation home to Carl, who has no creditors and, as long as he remembers to drive safely, is not likely to. Because Bill transferred the vacation home to Carl for the purpose of defeating a creditor, the transfer is a fraudulent conveyance. That means that the creditor, who otherwise had no claim against Carl, now does, i.e. a claim for the return of the vacation home.

As a general rule, California follows the rule of the non-community property states with respect to California *separate property.* In California, the creditor of a married person can access the community property, but cannot access the separate property of a non-debtor spouse.[12] But even here, there is an exception. The separate property of a married person can be accessed by the creditors of the other spouse if the creditor supplied the debtor-spouse with "necessities of life."[13] For example, if Carl runs up a tab at the corner grocery and then skips town, the grocer can get at Bill's separate property, because food, if anything, is a "necessity of life." But so might a hospital stay that runs up a tab of a few thousand dollars. This "necessaries of life" rule applies only for necessaries incurred by a spouse when still living with the other spouse. If the "necessaries" are incurred after the two

---

[12] Family Code §913.
[13] Family Code §914.

spouses are living apart – even if not under a legal separation – the "necessaries" exception does not apply.

The worst news here is that the debts – even the premarital debts – of one spouse can be visited upon the assets of the other spouse if the spouses have community property. But that does not mean that spouses are helpless. All of this can be changed by a premarital or post-marital agreement removing the spouses from community property. More on that in Chapter 2.

• *Liability for Debts upon Divorce.*

Most divorcing spouses, when they enter upon a divorce, focus primarily on how their assets are going to be divided. It's only later that they begin to focus on which assets are subject to the debts that were incurred during the marriage.

Fortunately, the rules here are a bit more intuitive than the rules contained in §910 of the Family Code. Let's assume that Bill and Carl get divorced. During their marriage, they have acquired community property, but each has his own separate property. The divorce court judge awards each of them his own separate property, and divides the community property equally, as the judge is required to do. There is, however, the small matter of Carl's liability on his personal guaranty. Which assets can Carl's creditors attach if they get a judgment against Carl? They can certainly attach Carl's separate property. They can also attach the one-half of the community property that Carl is assigned in the divorce. They cannot, however, attach Bill's separate property and cannot attach the one-half of the community property that Bill is assigned in the divorce, unless, as part of the divorce settlement, the debt is assigned to Bill.[14] This one fact substantially reduces the ability of a creditor to seize assets once married couples divorce. While the spouses are still married, a creditor can get at both halves of the community property. After the spouses have parted, the creditor of one spouse can attach only that spouse's separate property and the *half* of the community property assigned to that spouse.

There was some ambiguity as to exactly when community property ceases to be community property, but that ambiguity has been resolved by a recent case. In *Litke O'Farrell, LLC v. Tipton,*[15] one spouse was assigned certain assets in a marital settlement agreement ("MSA"). The creditor of the other spouse sought to attach the assets after the MSA had been entered into, but before the MSA had been approved by the divorce court judge, i.e. before the division of property became a court order. The Court of Appeals ruled that the assets were not subject to claims of the other spouse's creditors. They ceased to be community property when the MSA was entered into. An order of the court approving the MSA was not required.

- *Can you defeat a creditor by getting divorced?*

We have seen that the creditor of one spouse can seize both halves of the community property, but that if spouses divorce (or separate) that spouse's creditors can get at only that spouse's separate property and the one-half of the community property that is assigned to him or her. This distinction has resulted in a number of married couples getting divorced in order to defeat a creditor. If the divorce is contested, the judge must divide the community property

---

[14] Family Code §916(a).
[15] 204 Cal. App. 4th 1178 (2012).

equally. But if the divorce is "friendly," there is nothing that prevents the spouses from assigning the bulk of the community property to the non-debtor spouse, leaving the debtor spouse with very little for the creditor to go after. Once the settlement agreement is drawn up and signed, the judge will sign it, making it a court order and part of the judgment.

Does this work? Until recently, most attorneys in California assumed that it did work. After all, there is little that is stronger or more final than a judgment signed by a judge. But now we can't be sure. In 2003, the California Supreme Court decided *Mejia v. Reed*,[16] which stands for the proposition that a creditor can indeed overturn a marital settlement agreement if the creditor can prove that the division of property was motivated by the desire to defeat a creditor.

The facts in *Mejia v. Reed* are simple enough. Danilo Reed was married to Violeta Reed. Danilo had an extramarital affair with Rhina Mejia, which resulted in a child. Needless to say, Danilo was obligated to pay child support to Rhina. The issue was how much child support Danilo would be required to pay, which is a function of the payor's income and assets. So Danilo and Violeta got divorced. In their marital settlement agreement, Danilo conveyed all of the real estate that Danilo and Violeta owned to Violeta, leaving him with nothing. The marital settlement agreement was duly signed by the divorce court judge.

The issue for the California Supreme Court was whether the law regarding *fraudulent conveyances* can trump the provisions of the Family Code that says – as we

---

[16] 31 Cal. 4th 657.

have seen – that a creditor of a divorcing spouse can get at only that part of the community property that is assigned to that spouse. The Supreme Court held for Rhina, noting, famously, that:

> "...it is unlikely that the Legislature intended to grant married couples
> a one-time-only opportunity to defraud creditors by including the
> fraudulent transfer in an M[arital] S[ettlement] A[greement]."

As a result of *Mejia v. Reed*, every divorce lawyer must look over his or her shoulder every time assets are divided in a divorce, not knowing whether a creditor might have the ability to overturn a marital settlement agreement.

Which Spouse Controls Which Assets?

The fourth area where separate/community property matters is with respect to the management rights with respect to the property. This is generally not as important as the three other areas, and usually arises only when the spouses are divorcing and one spouse alleges that the other spouse either mismanaged or diverted community assets, and is now arguing for a reimbursement. But the rules are worth mentioning.

Generally, each spouse has the right to manage his or her separate property without interference from the other. Also as a general rule, both spouses have an equal right to manage the community property, which includes with it the right to be informed by the other spouse of any actions that spouse is taking with respect to the community property. Each spouse is considered a *fiduciary* of the community, i.e. owes a duty of trust to the community, and might be required to reimburse the other spouse if the spouse breached his or her fiduciary duty. In one case, the husband ran the family business, which was community property. But he put his girlfriend on the payroll. In the divorce that followed, he was required to reimburse the community for the community funds he dissipated in favor of his girlfriend.

A spouse may not give away community property or sell community property used in the home without the prior written consent of the other. That does not mean, however, that a spouse who did not know of the gift or the sale of the home furnishings could void the sale. It just means that the spouse could claim a reimbursement from the other in the event of a divorce.[17]

As always, there are some exceptions to the general rules. A spouse may not sell community real estate without the other spouse joining in, and if one spouse attempts to sell community real estate without informing the other, the other spouse could void the sale within one year of the date that the offending deed was recorded.[18] As a practical matter, this never happens. No purchaser of real estate will buy real estate from a married person unless the seller either represents that he or she is not married, and if married will require the non-signing spouse to disclaim any community property interest in the property. In addition, if two parties are residing in the separate property residence of one spouse, the spouse who owns the residence may not sell, mortgage or transfer the residence for the first three months after notice of the pendency of the divorce is recorded with the county clerk unless, of course, the other

---

[17] Family Code §1100(b) and (c).
[18] Family Code §1102(d).

spouse consents or the divorce court judge rules otherwise.[19]

The final exception exists with respect to family-owned businesses. The spouse who is in fact managing the business has the sole right to manage the business without the consent of the other spouse. The only "exception-to-the-exception" is if the managing spouse intends to dispose of all of the assets of the business, in which event the prior consent of the other spouse is required.[20]

Joint Tenants and Tenants-in-Common

If you don't want to get in the weeds on this stuff, you can skip this section, content in the knowledge that spouses can own property in California as their separate property or as community property.[21] But you won't know the whole story. When a parcel of property is owned by more than one person, married couples (and unmarried persons) can title their assets in *joint tenancy* or as *tenants in common*. They are very, very different, and whether you and your spouse will want to title your assets as tenancy-in-common or in joint tenancy will depend upon your wants and needs.

---

[19] Family Code §754.
[20] Family Code §1100(d).
[21] We have seen that there is a third category, *quasi-community property*, which is property a California couple acquires during marriage but which is located in a separate property state. It is treated for all purposes as community property.

Tenancy in Common

Let's assume that Sue Johnson and Sally Fisher bought a 20-acre farm outside of Oakland before they were married. They dipped into their joint bank account for the down payment, and every month they take part of their earnings to pay the mortgage. Twice a year, they pay the property taxes from their joint bank account. No one could doubt that the farm is their community property, with each of them owning a one-half interest in the community. The deed to the farm recites that the farm is owned "Sue Johnson and Sally Fisher, as tenants in common." If you guessed that that means that Sue and Sally each own 50% of the farm, you would be correct. But what does that mean? It does *not* mean that Sue owns 10 acres and Sally owns 10 acres. It does not mean that in the event of a divorce Sue gets 10 acres and Sally gets 10 acres (unless they enter into a settlement agreement to that effect.) It does mean that Sally and Sue each own an *undivided* 50% interest in the *entire* farm, which is a mind-blowing concept, but that's what it is.

As we have seen, since the farm is still community property, a creditor of either Sue or Sally could seize the entire farm to satisfy a judgment against either of them. But since Sue and Sally each own only half of the farm, if Sue writes a Will leaving the farm to her Uncle Eddie, Eddie will get only half the farm. Eddie will be a tenant-in-common with Sally.

Sue and Sally each owned a 50% tenancy-in-common interest in the farm. But they could have owned the farm in any proportion. If Sally had put up 10% of the down payment and Sue 90%, they could have taken title as

"Sally Fisher, as to a 10% interest, and Sue Johnson as to a 90% interest, as tenants in common." Unless they agree otherwise, Sally will get 10% of the income from the farm and Sue 90%, and when the farm is sold they will share the profits 90-10.

Joint Tenancy

Joint tenancy is often called "joint tenancy with right of survivorship." You may see it abbreviated on deeds and bank accounts as "JTWROS." "Right of survivorship" is not just an attribute of joint tenancy; it is the heart of soul of joint tenancy. It is to joint tenancy what white is to dove and black is to raven. You cannot have the one without the other.

Here, in a nutshell, is how "right of survivorship" works. Let's assume that Sue and Sally take title to the farm as "Sue Johnson and Sally Fisher, JTWROS." If Sue dies, Sally gets Sue's rights to the property. Technically, Sally had 100% of the property all along, *as did Sue!* Sally didn't get Sue's half of the property. Instead, Sue's interest in the property terminated with her death.

To prove the point, let's assume that Sue wrote a Will leaving her interest in the farm in equal shares to eight nephews, four nieces and the Los Angeles Dodgers. How much of the farm do the nieces, nephews and the Dodgers inherit? None of it. It all goes to Sally. Let's assume that Sue had no Will, but had three children of a prior marriage. How much of the farm do the children inherit? None of it. Sally, as Sue's joint tenant, becomes the sole owner of the farm because Sue's interest in the farm is extinguished by her death.

Joint tenancy is sometimes referred to as a "poor man's estate plan," because you can leave you assets to your intended beneficiaries by titling the assets in joint tenancy with those beneficiaries, without the necessity of a Will or a trust. The property will transfer automatically to the surviving joint tenant, without going through probate. There are, however, some tax disadvantages inherent in joint tenancy, which we will discuss in Chapter 4.

The right of survivorship is not the only significant difference between joint tenancy and tenancy-in-common. If a married couple own property as joint tenants in California, each spouse owns a one-half *separate property* interest in the property. Property in joint tenancy can never be community property. We saw earlier that §910 of the Family Code provides that a creditor of one spouse can go after both halves of the community property, which is the principal disadvantage of community property. But if property is titled in joint tenancy, a creditor of one spouse can attach only *half* of the separate property. In that event, the creditor would become a tenant in common with the other joint tenant.

Let's assume that that Sue and Sally owned the farm as joint tenants. In a year prior to Sue and Sally getting married, Sue failed to pay her taxes. The IRS assessed a tax deficiency against Sue, and recorded a *Notice of Federal Tax Lien* against the farm. If Sue and Sally wished to sell the farm, they would first have to retire Sue's tax debt before they could sell it. But let's assume that Sue died. What happens to the IRS' tax lien? It disappears, along with Sue's interest in the farm. Sally gets the entire farm (technically, she always owned the entire farm) free of Sue's tax lien, and free any other debt of Sue's.

There are some other differences between tenancy-in-common and joint tenancy. For one, you can hold any percentage interest as a tenant in common. But joint tenants must hold their interests equally. If spouses own property as joint tenants, each must own 50%. If there are three joint tenants, each must own a third. Secondly, you can dispose of an interest as a joint tenant without the consent of the other joint tenant(s), but the transferee cannot thereby become a joint tenant; he or she must be a tenant in common. This result stems from the rule that all joint tenants must come by their interest in the property at the same time and through the same instrument.

Tenancy-by-the-Entirety: Too bad we don't have it in California

We mention tenancy-by-the entirety here, even California doesn't have it, to illustrate the point that there are still hidden differences between the marriages of opposite-sex and same-sex couples.

Tenancy-by-the-entirety is a form of property ownership reserved to married couples. The key to tenancy-by-the-entirety is that if property is titled as such, the tenancy cannot be severed by one spouse without the consent of the other spouse. The effect of this is that if only one of two spouses is indebted to a creditor, and that creditor obtains a judgment against that spouse, the creditor cannot get at the property as long as the marriage persists. Of course, every marriage eventually ends, either through divorce or death, but most creditors aren't willing to wait that long. Tenancy-by-the-entirety puts the debtor in the driver's seat when it comes to negotiating a settlement of the debt.

There are approximately 25 states that have tenancy-by-the-entirety in one form or another. None of the community property states do. Most limit it to real estate, and some only to the marital residence. A few, however, permit any asset to be titled in tenancy-by-the entirety.

We don't have tenancy-by-the-entirety in California. But that doesn't mean that California married couples cannot own property in states that do, and it is here we encounter yet another difference between opposite-sex and same-sex couples. If a married California opposite-sex couple acquires property in a tenancy-by-the-entirety state, it is likely that the state in which the property is located will give the California couple the same protection as it would married couples in the home state. But let's assume that a California same-sex couple acquires property in a tenancy-by-the-entirety state. If that state is one of the 35 other states that provide for same-sex marriage, it's likely that state will give the California couple the same protection that it gives its own same-sex couples. But if the state does not honor same-sex marriage, it is highly unlikely that the state will honor an attempt by a California same-sex couple to title the asset as tenancy-the-the-entirety, and will not protect the asset if a creditor attempts to seize it.

Chapter 2
Premarital (and Post-Marital) Agreements

Introduction

If everything you have read in Chapter 1 leaves you feeling a little queasy, you're not alone. If you intend to keep what you owned prior to getting married after you're married, you have a problem. As we have seen, even though the property you owned prior to marriage is separate property, it's easy to commingle separate and community property. It's also easy for a spouse to build up a community property interest in the other's separate property if the spouse devotes time and effort – a community "asset" – in the development and maintenance of that spouse's separate property. What is worse, even if the spouses remain happily married forever, if one of the spouses develops a creditor, that creditor can get at both halves of the community property. What is perhaps worst is that a spouse's wages, salary and any other compensation earned during the marriage is community property, subject to the creditors of the other spouse.

There's got to be a way out from under all of this, and, of course, there is, with a valid premarital agreement, also known as a *prenuptial agreement*. Already married? No worries, mate. California permits spouses to enter into a post-marital agreement, which the governing statute calls a *transmutation agreement*, which provides for the "transmutation" of community property into separate property. More on that shortly.

Premarital agreements have followed a long and tortuous history in California. Our legislature enacted a statute authorizing premarital agreements as early as 1850, the year California was granted statehood. But the law took a radical turn in 2001, in response to the California Supreme Court's infamous decision following Barry Bonds' divorce.

Barry Bonds Gets Married – And Divorced

Long before his heroics with the San Francisco Giants, and even longer before his issues with performance-enhancing drugs, Barry Bonds was a 23-year old outfielder with the Pittsburgh Pirates earning $106,000 a year.

In the summer of 1987 Bonds met a Swede named Susann (known as "Sun") who was living in Montreal. In October, 1988, he invited her to visit him at his home in Phoenix, Arizona. She moved in the next month, and shortly thereafter they became engaged. In January, 1988, they decided to marry before spring training. On February 5, 1988, Sun and Barry entered into a premarital agreement in which each waived any interest in the property or earnings of the other throughout their marriage. At the time, Sun was unemployed, and would remain unemployed throughout their marriage. Later on February 5, 1988, Sun and Barry flew to Las Vegas. They were married the next day. Sun and Barry were divorced in 1994. They had two children.

That much we know for sure. The rest is the subject of contradictory recollections of what was said and not said surrounding the execution of the premarital agreement. There is some ambiguity as to how well Sun understood English and how well she understood Barry. According to Barry, he told her right from the start of the relationship that he wished to avoid the acrimonious divorces he had witnessed in some of his teammates, which they would avoid with a premarital agreement providing for "what's mine is mine; what's yours is yours," and that Sun had agreed. Sun, on the other hand, had no recollection of ever discussing money or property with Barry.

Sun testified that only on the night preceding the signing of the premarital agreement did Barry mention that they needed to go to his lawyer to sign a prenuptial agreement the following day. She also testified that Barry's financial advisor told her, while in the parking lot of the lawyer's office, that if she did not sign the premarital agreement, there would be no wedding the following day. She remembered all of this being very rushed, because they did not wish to miss the plane waiting to fly them to Las Vegas. She was not put off by the mention of the premarital agreement. She believed (or so she testified) that she thought that the premarital agreement dealt only with the property of each at the time of the marriage. In fact, the premarital agreement contained the following:

"We agree that all of the earnings and accumulations resulting from the
other's personal services, skill efforts and work, together with all
property acquired with funds and income derived therefrom, shall be
the separate property of that spouse."

Significantly, Sun did not recall anyone telling her she had the right to consult with her own attorney or that if there were no premarital agreement, she would have a right to half of Barry's earnings in the event of a divorce. Whatever concerns she had were limited to missing the flight to Las Vegas.

Needless to say, the recollections of Barry and his attorneys were very different. They recalled that Sun was advised that Barry's lawyers represented only him, not her, and that she did indeed have the right to her own lawyer. They recalled having read the premarital agreement to her, paragraph by paragraph, and that at no time did anyone threaten to cancel the wedding if she did not sign.

There is one more salient fact. The court noted that the wedding itself was a rather small, informal affair. There was no caterer, no printed invitations, and only a few guests were invited, all of whom were relatives or friends of Barry, including his godfather, Willie Mays. Of what possible relevance could this be? It goes to the issue of *duress*. If the wedding had been a typical wedding-planner blowout, with calligraphied invitations, maids of honor, flowers, an orchestra and scores of guests, backing out at the last minute would have been such an embarrassment that Sun would have had no choice but to sign anything just to assure that the wedding went forward. The court held that backing out would have caused her little embarrassment.

The case followed a tortured route through the California courts. The trial court held in Barry's favor. The California Court of Appeals reversed, voiding the premarital agreement. Barry appealed. The California Supreme Court, in *In re Marriage of Bonds,*[22] held in Barry's favor, to the effect that, considering all of the testimony, the agreement was entered into voluntarily.

In re Marriage of Bonds is a template for the hundreds, if not thousands, of cases that do not feature

---

[22] 24 Cal. 4th 1 (2000).

litigants as famous as Barry Bonds and which do not make it to the California Supreme Court. But in one respect, these cases are all the same. They all involve a deep-pocket spouse wishing to uphold the premarital agreement against his or her impecunious spouse wishing to overturn it on the grounds of fraud, duress, lack of capacity or a combination of all three. In every case, the recollections of what was said at the time the agreement was entered into vary greatly.

The response of the California legislature to *In re Marriage of Bonds* was to say, in effect, "enough." No more premarital agreements signed on the tarmac while the plane waiting to take bride and groom to the wedding has its engines running.

What a Premarital Agreement Can (and Cannot) Do

Section 1500 of the California Family Code provides:

"The property rights of husband and wife prescribed by statute may be
altered by a premarital agreement or other marital property agreement."

In other words, California says to couples contemplating marriage in California that if you don't want to have community property, you don't have to have it. If you don't want your spouse's creditors (including the ones whose claims preceded the marriage) to be able to get at your wages, no problem, you can fix that with a premarital agreement.

What can you do with a premarital agreement? The most important thing is that you can remove yourself from community property. You can provide (as Barry and Sun Bonds did) that in the event of a divorce, property that is titled in one person's name is that person's separate property, and that nothing that either party does with respect to that property can change that.[23] With a valid premarital agreement no one (including the creditor of a spouse) can ever argue that a spouse built up a community property interest in the assets of the other spouse as a result of the time and effort that the spouse devoted to the asset. But you may not wish to remove yourself entirely from community property. You may wish to provide that only the property that each spouse owns at the time of the marriage will remain separate property, with no possibility of the other spouse building up a community property interest in those assets, while permitting community property for after-acquired assets and/or wages and salaries earned during the marriage.

You may, in a premarital agreement, specify who will get what in the event of a divorce, but here you need to be a bit careful. If the premarital agreement wires in a cash bonus to one spouse in a divorce that is so great that the bonus could be deemed to be an inducement to a divorce, a court might refuse to uphold the premarital agreement based on the theory that California's public policy is to foster marriages, not destroy them.

You may, in a premarital agreement, specify who will get what assets in the event of a spouse's death. Remember, if a person writes a Will, that person can freely

---

[23] Family Code §1612(a)(1). Sections 1600 – 1617 of the Family Code represent California's version of the Uniform Premarital Agreement Act. California was the first state to adopt this statute.

tear up the Will at any time during that person's lifetime. The beneficiaries under that Will have no vested right to anything in a Will until the testator dies, at which point the Will becomes irrevocable. But you can change this result with a provision in a premarital agreement that requires a spouse to write a Will (or trust) leaving certain assets to the other spouse, a provision that is enforceable against other beneficiaries if the spouse changes the Will prior to death.

You may, in a premarital agreement, provide for – and waive – a right to *spousal support*, a/k/a alimony. But here you must be very careful. Section 1612(c) of the Family Code, a provision that has Barry Bonds' fingerprints all over it, states that any provision contained in a premarital agreement regarding spousal support is not enforceable if the party against whom it is to be enforced (the person whose interest it is to have the agreement found invalid) was not represented by independent legal counsel at the time that the agreement was signed, or if the provision waiving or limiting spousal support is "unconscionable" at the time it is to be enforced, i.e. at the time of divorce. Moreover, if a waiver of spousal support turns out to be unconscionable, being represented by independent legal counsel doesn't salvage it.

The legal counsel representing each side to a premarital agreement should be truly "independent." Advising your fiancé to "Visit attorney Joe Brown, and have him send me the bill" is playing with fire. Let your fiancé find his or her own attorney.

Even if both parties to a premarital agreement are represented by independent legal counsel, it is possible that a divorce court judge may one day refuse to uphold a waiver of spousal support if the court finds that the passage of time has rendered the waiver unconscionable. Two recent cases prove the point. In *Marriage of Factor*[24] the court refused to uphold a complete waiver of spousal support where the parties had been married for 16 years and the wife, with the husband's consent, remained a full-time housewife throughout the marriage. The "unconscionability" stems from the fact that the wife pursued no education throughout the marriage, rendering it impossible for her to replicate the standard of living she enjoyed during the marriage. Similarly, in *Marriage of Melissa*[25] the court refused to uphold a complete waiver of spousal support where the wife did not work outside the home throughout the 20-year marriage, devoting many years to the care of a disabled child.

These cases suggest that it is unwise (or at least dangerous) to write a total waiver of spousal support into a premarital agreement. These cases require that a premarital agreement contain a *severability clause*, which states that the balance of a premarital agreement will be upheld if any one provision – such as the waiver of spousal maintenance – is held unenforceable.

What You Cannot Do

There are certain things that you cannot do in a premarital agreement, no matter how many independent attorneys bless it. Here is a short list:

- *You cannot waive child support.* You cannot write a premarital agreement that says that, in the event of a divorce, one party is absolved from paying child support, or is limited to paying only a certain dollar amount

---

[24] 212 C.A. 4th 967 (2013).
[25] 212 CA 4th 598 (2012).

of child support. The reason that all of these provisions are voidable is that the right to receive child support doesn't belong to the parent, it belongs to the child, and a spouse cannot waive a right the spouse does not own.

• *You cannot waive your right to support during the marriage.* You may waive your right to receive spousal support after the marriage has ended, but you cannot waive your right to support during the marriage. Each spouse in California owes the other a duty of "mutual respect, fidelity and support."[26] You cannot waive it.

• *You cannot agree to raise your children in a particular religion.* You can write a premarital agreement that includes a provision to the effect that the children will be raised as Methodists, but no court will enforce it.

• *"Fault" provisions are unenforceable.* California has long had a policy of "no fault" divorce. There are no "grounds" for divorce, and if one spouse alleges that the marriage is broken, it is. Except insofar as it relates to child custody, no one cares whether one spouse was "cheating" on the other, was a drunk or a kleptomaniac. Similarly, a divorce court will not uphold a provision in a premarital agreement that seeks to penalize a spouse if the spouse commits adultery, or any other "fault."

Ensuring that a Premarital Agreement Will be Enforced

In 2001, as a result of the Legislature's revulsion at the California Supreme Court's decision in the Barry Bonds case, the Legislature essentially nullified that case. The

---

[26] Family Code §720.

result was a substantial tightening of the rules for enforcement of premarital agreements. In general, the Legislature sought to ensure that any person who signs a premarital agreement does so *voluntarily*. To ensure that, the Legislature required that, in all future premarital agreements:

• The party desiring to invalidate the agreement must have been represented by independent legal counsel at the time of the premarital agreement or, after having been advised to seek independent counsel, expressly waived the right to independent counsel in a separate document, i.e. in a document other than the premarital agreement itself.[27] Remember: If the premarital agreement contains a waiver of spousal support, each side must be represented by independent counsel; a waiver of the right to independent counsel won't do.

Once again, independent counsel must be truly independent, or you run the risk that the agreement will not be enforced. Handing your intended spouse with the name and address of a lawyer and paying the lawyer's bill will likely result in the divorce court not enforcing the agreement.

• The party against whom enforcement is sought must have had *seven calendar days* between the time that the party was first presented with the premarital agreement and advised to seek independent counsel and the time that the agreement was signed.[28] This prevents a party

---

[27] Family Code §1615(c)(1).

[28] Family Code §1615(c)(2).

from being first presented with the premarital agreement in the limo on the way to the wedding.

• If a party is not represented by independent legal counsel, he or she must be informed of the basic effects of the agreement and the rights that he or she is giving up by signing the agreement. Needless to say, the party must be proficient in the language in which the agreement (and the explanation of the waiver of rights) is being prepared. If the intended spouse speaks only Armenian, it is not sufficient to provide that spouse with an attorney who speaks Armenian review the provisions of the agreement. In such a case, it is essential that the agreement, and any explanation of the rights being waived, be translated into Armenian, and the Armenian-speaking attorney should then review the translation with the client. As a further precaution, the attorney should sign a declaration to the effect that he or she faithfully translated the agreement into Armenian and reviewed the translation with the client. This may sound like overkill, but it isn't. The last thing you want to do is give a divorce court judge a "hook" for not enforcing a premarital agreement.

Even before the adoption of the Uniform Premarital Agreement Act in 2001, parties needed to be careful that a premarital agreement could be avoided by an allegation by the party against whom enforcement was sought that he or she was *fraudulently induced* to sign the agreement as a result of the other party not fully disclosing all of his or her assets. Here's how that works: The premarital agreement contains the usual waivers, either of community property or spousal support or both. The agreement contains a list of each party's assets and liabilities. Mr. Bigbucks, however, fails to list an apartment building that he owns that is worth $2 million. In the divorce, Mr. Bigbucks seeks to enforce the premarital agreement. Mrs. Bigbucks alleges that had she known of the existence of the apartment building, she never would have signed the premarital agreement. Now Mr. Bigbucks is sorry he never mentioned this asset. General rule: Never, never, ever omit an asset from the disclosures that are appended to the premarital agreement. We also advise that each page of the financial disclosures be separately signed or initialed, so as to ensure that many years later – during the divorce – no party can allege that someone altered a page or inserted a page. You cannot be too careful.

Post-Marital Agreements

Already married? No premarital agreement? As we have seen, there is a presumption that all of your assets are community property, and to the extent that an asset is community property, one spouse's creditors can seize the entire asset. Is there a solution?

Yes. California allows for post-marital agreements, allowing already-married spouses to *transmute* their community property into separate property, or, if they would like, to transmute their separate property into community property (we don't see too many of these.) These post-marital agreements are known as *transmutation agreements* and, like premarital agreements, are governed by a statute, §850 of the Family Code.

Unlike premarital agreements, there are very few rules governing transmutation agreements. The reason is that when two people negotiate a pre-marital agreement, they stand before each other as legal strangers, negotiating a contract like any other commercial contract. Other than the duty not to commit fraud, they owe each other nothing. That's why the Legislature felt that it needed to protect all of the Sun Bonds of the world from all of the Barry Bonds of the world. But when two people are already married and set out to enter into a transmutation agreement, each owes a legal duty of trust and a duty to engage in fair dealing to the other.

One of the rules that governs transmutation agreements is the requirement that if real estate is transmuted, the transmutation is effective against creditors only if notice of the transmutation is given. So we record a memorandum of the transmutation agreement, informing anyone who wishes to check the title that a parcel of real property that was once owned by Julie Johnson and Jodie Johnson as their community property is now the separate property of Julie alone.[29]

There is one huge limitation with respect to transmutation agreements. Section 851 of the Family Code provides: "A transmutation is subject to the laws governing fraudulent transfers." What does that mean? Hard to say. But let's assume that Julie Johnson and Jodie Johnson are spouses. Julie is a surgeon. Jodie is a homemaker. They own a home in Los Angeles that has substantial equity, own mutual funds titled in their names, and have a substantial balance in the bank. All of their assets are community property. Then one day Julie is sued for malpractice, having deposited one more surgical pad into a patient than she removed prior to closing up the patient. So the day after the lawsuit is filed Julie and Jodie enter into a transmutation agreement. They transmute the home, the mutual funds and the bank account to Jodie as her separate property, and leave Julie with $12.40 as her separate property. Fraudulent conveyance? Probably. People don't give up their community property interest in hundreds of

---

[29] Family Code §852.

thousands (if not millions) in assets unless they wish to defeat a creditor.

But that doesn't mean that Julie and Jodie cannot enter into a transmutation agreement after the lawsuit is filed. It just means that they need to be careful. If Julie and Jodie each emerge from the transmutation agreement with a separate property interest in assets equaling the value of the assets in which the other has a separate property interest, it's going be difficult for a creditor to allege that the transfers were fraudulent conveyances. Each received a separate property interest in assets equal to the community property interests in assets ceded to the other. Of course, this doesn't solve Julie's problem; it solves only half the problem, with the assets in which Julie received a separate property interest still exposed to creditors.

That's the theory. But in practice, a transmutation agreement may shield far more than half the assets. The reason is that while certain assets have an ascertainable fair market value, they are of no value to a creditor seizing the asset. For example, Julie's medical practice undoubtedly has a value subject to an appraisal. If Julie wished to retire, she could probably sell the practice to another surgeon. But Julie's practice has no value to a creditor, other than the cash, the accounts receivable and the equipment located in the office. The real value of Julie's medical practice, the goodwill of the practice, has no value to a creditor.

Chapter 3
Income Tax Planning for Same-Sex Couples

Introduction

One thing that every same-sex couple in California knew before *United States v. Windsor* was decided was that they didn't need to concern themselves over how they filed their taxes. In the eyes of the Internal Revenue Service, same-sex couples were total strangers, and each partner was required to file his or her federal income tax return as a single person.

That's all changed. Following the Supreme Court's decision is *Windsor*, the IRS made a complete about-face, ruling that same-sex couples *must* file their federal income taxes either as "married filing jointly," (which is, by far, the most common practice) or "married filing separately." Filing as single persons, as they did before, is not an option. Moreover, if a same-sex couple is legally married in a state – such a California -- that recognizes same-sex marriages, and the couple then moves to a state that does not recognize same-sex marriages, the couple must still file their federal income tax returns as either married filing jointly or as married filing separately. This can produce some strange results, in light of the fact that married same-sex couples residing in a state that does not recognize their marriage will likely be required to file their *state* income tax returns as if they were single!

The IRS has also ruled that *Windsor* did not change the status of same-sex couples who are not married but who are in some form of "civil union" permitted under state law. In California, many same-sex couples become Registered

Domestic Partners prior to the Supreme Court's decision in *Windsor*. These Registered Domestic Partners cannot file joint federal tax returns, despite the fact that they can file their California *state* tax returns on a joint basis.

Marriage Penalty or Marriage Benefit?

Will a newly-married California same-sex couple see their income taxes increase or decrease as a result of the requirement that they file their federal tax returns as a married couple? In other words, will the married couple suffer a "penalty" or reap a benefit as a result of their new filing status? It depends. As a general rule, if only one of the two spouses earns an income, or if their income is widely disparate, the couple will reap a benefit from filing jointly. If both spouses earn a high income that is roughly equal, they will find that that their joint tax liability will be greater than when they were required to file separately – a marriage penalty.

Here's why: Contrary to popular belief, your income taxes are not computed based on a single rate of tax. Instead, your taxes are the result of a blend of rates. The first dollars you earn in a given year are taxed at a lower rate. As your income increases throughout the year, you pass through ever-higher tax brackets. For example, if a married couple earns $90,000 in a given year, the first $36,900 is taxed at a $15% rate. Everything up to $89,150 is taxed at a 28% rate, and the last $850 is taxed at a 31% rate. But a single person reaches the higher brackets at lower levels of income. A single person hits the 28% bracket when he or she earns the first dollar over $22,100, and hits the 31% bracket when he or she earns the first dollar over $53,500. The result is that if only one spouse earns income, that spouse is taxed as if that spouse were a single person, but with more advantageous marginal tax rates.

Aside from the possibility of a marriage benefit resulting from the difference in tax rates, being married carries with it a number of income tax benefits unavailable to single taxpayers. For example, many employers offer health insurance benefits to their employees and their employees' spouses. If an employee purchased health insurance for a "spouse" in a state that does not recognize same-sex marriage, the value of the policy was considered a taxable benefit. In the employee bought a policy for an opposite-sex spouse, the policy was treated as a non-taxable benefit.

In addition to income tax benefits, there are social security benefits available to a surviving or divorced spouse. Needless to say, no such social security benefits are available to same-sex couples who are not married. But there is a flip side to this coin. Many same-sex couples were in opposite-sex marriages that ended in divorce. Once a divorced or surviving spouse remarries, either to a same-sex or heterosexual partner, those social security benefits are lost.

There are tax detriments to being married, aside from the marriage penalty, if the spouses have relatively equal incomes. The effect of combining incomes on a joint will often result in higher taxable income, resulting in the phase-out or loss of tax benefits. For example, it may result in a spouse being unable to contribute to a Roth I.R.A., even though that spouse could contribute to the Roth I.R.A. before his or her income was combined with that of the spouse. Similarly, the Child Tax Credit – a $1,000 for each child under age 17 – begins to phase out when a married couple has $11,000 of adjusted gross income, a level which is easier to reach if the married couple files jointly. A person may claim the "adoption tax credit" which is a tax credit for the expenses incurred in adopting a child. But no such credit is available if you adopt a spouse's child. In addition, even if the adoption credit is available, it phases out once you reach a level of adjusted gross income of $194,580. If you are considering adopting your spouse's child, you should consider doing it – and incurring the expenses related to it – prior to actually getting married.

Amend Your Prior Returns?

If you feel that you suffered a marriage penalty for all of the years that you resided in California prior to *United States v. Windsor* but were unable to marry, can you go back and amend your federal income tax returns? Yes, you can. But you can amend only for the three prior tax years. For example, you have until April 15, 2015 to amend your 2011 tax return, and April 15, 2016 to amend the 2012 tax year, and so forth. Of course, you are not required to amend your prior returns. If you and your spouse "crunch the numbers" and believe that you overpaid your taxes by filing separate returns in the years that are still open, you can now file a joint return on Form 1040X. Some people believe that filing an amended return increases the risk of an audit. The IRS has advised its agents not to audit amended returns that are filed solely to change the filing status. Advise your return preparer to write: "Filed Pursuant to Revenue Ruling 2013-17" on the top of the amended return. That's the IRS ruling that permits same-sex couples to amend their returns to reflect their new filing status.

Taxes and Separated Same-Sex Couples

Same-sex couples have been cleared to marry only since June, 2013, so it's a little early to start thinking about the separations and divorces of those same-sex couples. But it is a certainty that many same-sex couples will separate and divorce, just as opposite-sex couples do.

We noted earlier that married couples must file their federal taxes either as married filing jointly or as married filing separately. Generally, married couples prefer to file jointly, because the tax bill will be lower than if they file separately, regardless of who earns the income. But many married couples have no choice but to file separately, for the simple reason that they are separated. That does not present a problem if the spouses live in a separate property state; each will report and pay tax on his or her income. But if the spouses reside in a community property state, their income may well be community property, and things get complicated.

As a general rule, if married but separated spouses do not file a joint return, each spouse is required file and report one-half of the community income, and pay the tax on that one-half of the income. Of course, each spouse is required to report and pay the tax on any separate income. But this rule can be harsh (indeed, impossible) for many separated spouses who have no way of knowing how much – if any – community income there is to report.

Along comes §66 of the Tax Code, which provides separated couples with some help. The IRS says that §66 is not a relief provision, but is "intended to protect abandoned spouses."

As a result, the §66 rules are tight, but here they are. If spouses were married to each other at any time during the year, and live apart <u>throughout</u> the entire year, and do not file a joint return, then they are exempt from the general rule that certain (but not all) community income must be reported one-half by each spouse. Instead, if one of the spouses had "earned income," (wages, salaries, etc) the spouse that provided the services that produced the income reports all of the income and pays the tax thereon. Similarly, income from a trade or business is taxed only to the spouse who exercised substantially all of the management and control of the business during the year. Also, if the spouses received distributions from a partnership, the partner who is the named partner reports the income and pays the tax.

Section 66 relief applies only if the spouses live apart throughout the entire year. The IRS says that "living apart" means that each spouse must have had a separate residence throughout the year. Jill requiring Jack to sleep in the basement doesn't count.

Unfortunately, not all community income is eligible for this relief. If dividends, interest income, rental income, gains from the sale of assets or royalty income are received, each spouse is required to report half of the income on his or her separate return. Of course, if one spouse "abandoned" the other, and the departing spouse later received dividends, it is unlikely that the abandoned spouse would ever learn of it. Here, too, §66 provides an out. Section 66(c) exempts a spouse from reporting community income if he or she can prove to the Treasury that he or she did not know of the income, and that "taking into account all of the facts and circumstances, it is inequitable to include such item of community income in such individual's gross income."

Complicating §66 further is that it treats "community" income only as that income earned while a person is "domiciled" in a community property state. "Domicile" does not mean "residence." "Domicile" is the place that, deep in your heart, you believe is your permanent home, the place you intend to return to when you are not there. You can have more than one residence, but only one domicile. For example, if you and your spouse live in California but your California employer sends you to Bolivia for two years, your income in Bolivia is community income, regardless of whether Bolivia has a community property regime or not. Conversely, a separated taxpayer who lives in Arkansas (a separate property state) but who earns income in California while on temporary assignment does not have community income and is not subject to §66.

A spouse cannot qualify for §66 relief if one spouse transferred income to the other spouse during the year. However, the IRS has made it clear that transferring income from one spouse to the other for the benefit of the spouses' child doesn't disqualify the spouses from using §66.

We noted earlier that the IRS now requires same-sex couples to file their returns either as married filing jointly or married filing separately, even if they were married in a state that recognized same-sex marriage and now reside in a state that does not. The same rules apply for separated same-sex couples. If they are separated but still married at year's end, they may file joint returns or as married filing separately. A spouse who qualifies may file as a "head of household." But they cannot file as single persons for the simple reason that they are not.

We saw in Chapter 2 that it is possible for California spouses to remove themselves from community property by entering into a prenuptial agreement prior to marriage or a transmutation agreement after marriage. If spouses make their incomes separate, as well as their assets, then §66 cannot apply to them. Each separated spouse will report and pay the tax on his or her separate income.

A Word About Registered Domestic Partners

When the courts overturned Proposition 8, it cleared the way for same-sex couples to marry. Many of these couples had previously registered to become "Registered Domestic Partners." It is likely that most of these "RDP's" will marry but some, for whatever reason, will elect to remain RDP's. As RDP's they will continue to live in a tax and non-tax netherworld of conflicting rules.

From a tax perspective, RDP's are treated as married persons for all California tax purposes, but are treated as unmarried single persons for all federal income tax purposes. That means that California RDP's must file joint returns, but may not file joint federal returns. That can – and will – produce some weird anomalies. For example, federal law permits married couples to exclude $500,000 of capital gain from the sale of a principal residence, but only $250,000 if a single person sells a residence. California provides the same exclusions. California thus provides the same $500,000 exclusion when RDP's sell a residence, but under federal law, the RDP's are considered two single individuals. Similarly, federal law provides certain tax benefits to the spouses of married taxpayers, such as the ability to exclude employer-provided accident and health insurance from income. No such federal benefit extends to RDP's. But on their state returns, California RDP's may exclude these benefits from income, because for state tax purposes RDP's are treated the same as married couples.

We saw in Chapter 1 that a divorcing spouse may access the other spouse's retirement plan by obtaining a Qualified Domestic Relations Order ("QDRO"). But that right arises from a federal statute. A divorcing California RDP would have no such right, even if the Supreme Court decides that a state cannot prohibit same-sex marriages.

Chapter 4
Estate Planning for Same-Sex Couples

Introduction: Why Plan Your Estate?

You don't have to. No one can force you to. But if a California resident dies without having done any estate planning, we often have some bad news for the survivors.

It has happened so often that we can relate to you almost exactly how the initial telephone goes, when a child or sibling of the departed calls us and tells us that mom or dad or sis has died. The first thing we ask is whether the deceased had a trust or a Will.

"No, nothing. Dad didn't believe much in lawyers. He also thought that stuff was mainly for rich people. All he owned was the house and a few checking accounts anyway."

At this point, even though we don't actually put down the receiver and get down on the floor and assume the prayer position, we arenow in prayer mode.

"How was the house titled?"

"Just in dad's name."

"How much was in the checking accounts?

"Altogether, $234,617"

We now have to impart the bad news. Dad's estate will have to be *probated*. No one will get his or her hands on the house or any of the money in the checking accounts unless and until someone gets an order from the *probate court*. That will take many months. And it will cost. How much it will cost will depend on the size of the "estate" but you can figure on 3-5% of the estate. And this is not the result of not having a Will. It is the result of not having a *trust*.

When it comes to estate planning, California same-sex couples are no different than opposite-sex couples. In fact, they are no different than unmarried people. If you plan ahead, your assets pass smoothly, quickly and cheaply to the people you want to receive them. If you don't plan, they may have an expensive, time-consuming mess.

All About Probate

Probate is not a mystery to anyone who has had a loved one who died and whose estate had to go through the probate process. But for most people, the probate process is something that they know they need to avoid, are not sure how to avoid it, and don't really know what it is. We have heard any number of people through the years tell uss that they don't need to worry about probate, because they have wills. If you have a will (but not a trust) you avoid a mess, but you don't avoid probate. If fact, the term "probate" means "proving" – the will! It is only with a pinto which title to all of the asset have been placed that we are assured of completely avoiding probate. More on that shortly. All mysteries are dispelled right here. Guaranteed.

Let's assume you write a will. It leaves your condo to your life partner, your golf clubs to your sister, your half of your business to your business partner, and your stock portfolio to your brother. The will is like a recipe, a directive. But there is one thing that your will cannot do: it cannot actually transfer the title to the condo. It cannot endorse the stock certificates that comprise the stock portfolio to your brother.

Were you alive, and you wished to transfer the condo, you would draw up a deed, sign it, notarize it, have it recorded, and your life partner would own the condo. But once you have died, you cannot reach up out of the grave and sign a deed transferring the condo. You cannot endorse the stock certificates to your brother. Someone else needs to do those things. That "someone" is the probate court, and the process of effecting the actual physical transfer of assets from a deceased person to the person's chosen beneficiaries is what the "probate" process is.

If probate is nothing more than transferring assets from a deceased person to the living people, what's the problem? In some states, it isn't much of a problem, and can be accomplished at little expense within a period of weeks. In other states – such as California – the simple process of transferring assets from a deceased person to living people can be downright Dickensian, involving petitions, appraisals, motions, court appearances, inventories, more hearings, more petitions, until a year and five to eight percent of the value of the estate has been consumed, until finally the beneficiaries receive the assets they were intended to receive. Fortunately, probate is everywhere avoidable with a *living trust* to which title to the assets have been transferred before the decedent dies.

What makes probate so complicated – and expensive? For starters, the court has to be convinced that the person who was nominated by the person who wrote the will (the *decedent*) to handle the estate (the *personal representative* or the *executor*) is a fit and proper person. The probate court will also want to assure itself that the written will actually represents the decedent's intent. Why wouldn't it? Let's assume that Mr. Brown had three children, but he left everything to only one of his children, Fred. The will looks O.K., properly witnessed and/or notarized in accordance with state law. Why shouldn't Fred receive everything? Perhaps if Mr. Brown's other children were to appear in court, they might shed some light on the matter. They might testify that Mr. Brown was in a wheelchair, and every morning when Fred took his father on their morning stroll, he threatened to release the wheelchair and his father over a cliff if his father didn't name Fred as the sole beneficiary. Mr. Brown told his two other children that he was terrified of Fred. In other words, Mr. Brown's will was the product of *duress*. Sound farfetched? We can assure you that as you read this page, there are scores of disappointed heirs in America who are at this moment consulting with their attorneys, preparing to challenge wills on the basis of duress, fraud or some other cause.

Even if the will is perfectly fine and all the beneficiaries are satisfied, there are any number of things that could delay the distribution of the assets to the beneficiaries. For starters, there is the matter of *creditors* of the estate. Mr. Brown's three children may be the designated beneficiaries of Mr. Brown's estate, but what they are entitled to get is only net of Mr. Brown's debts. If he owes on his credit cards, the mortuary, or the doctors who attended him during his last illness, they need to be paid first. One creditor who is certain to wish to be paid is the IRS, which understandably wants the income taxes that Mr. Brown owes for the last year of his life. So all of the creditors need to be notified, and given the opportunity to present their claims. How much time they have varies from state to state. If the administrator contests any of these claims, it will certainly delay the distribution of the assets to the children.

Which Assets are Subject to the Probate Process?

Not all assets need to go through probate. Some assets pass quickly and automatically to designated beneficiaries without the assistance of the probate court. Most of these assets have one thing in common: they are contractual affairs in which the contract names a designated beneficiary.

The most common asset that does not go through probate (and hence is not part of the "probate estate") is life insurance. If the "insured" dies, the designated beneficiaries of the insurance policy – which is a contract between the owner of the insurance policy and the insurance company – receive the insurance proceeds. Usually all that the insurance company requires in order to pay the insurance proceeds to the named beneficiaries is a death certificate. Similarly, the designated beneficiaries of a retirement plan, IRA, 401(k) plan and all other pension plans don't go through probate for the same reason that life insurance does not: they are contractual arrangements with named beneficiaries.

It's sometimes not easy to tell whether or not an asset needs to go through probate in order for the beneficiaries to receive the asset. Let's assume that Mr. Brown owned 100 shares of Ford Motor Company stock. In his will, he left the Ford stock to his son, Fred. Following Mr. Brown's death, if Fred were to present himself with a copy of the will to Ford's stock transfer agent, would the transfer agent issue a new share certificate for 100 Ford shares to Fred? Not a chance in the world. They would say to Fred, in effect: "Get an order from the probate court authorizing us to issue 100 shares to you, and we will do it." Mr. Brown's Ford stock is now part of the "probate estate."

But let's assume that the 100 shares that Mr. Brown owned were not shares of Ford Motor Company, but of "Brown-Schmidlapp Motors," a local car repair business owned by Mr. Brown and his partner, Syd Schmidlapp." The will leaves all of Fred Brown's shares to Syd. Must we go through the probate court in order to transfer Fred's 100 shares of Brown-Schmidlapp Motors to Syd? Not if none of Fred's heirs object. Fred and Syd probably have a "Brown-Schmidlapp Motors" stock book in the back of a file cabinet collecting dust. All Syd and Fred's executor need to do is tear up Fred's certificate, issue a new certificate to Syd, fill in the stock transfer ledger, and they're done.

There is one last asset that also avoids probate: joint tenancy. We saw in Chapter 1 that when property is titled in joint tenancy, and one joint tenant dies, the surviving joint tenant automatically accedes to the ownership of the entire asset. That's why property titled in joint tenacy does not go through probate.

How Living Trusts Avoid Probate

We now know that joint tenancy, life insurance, and retirement plans avoid probate. So do privately held assets such as the stock of small businesses. But what of all of the other assets, such as the Ford Motor Company stock and the real estate? How does a living trust avoid the probate of these assets?

Let's go back and remember just what it is that the probate process does. It handles the physical transfer of assets from a deceased person to the living people. When we create a trust, that trust is a separate "person." When we create a living trust, we do now, at our leisure, at little expense, what the probate court does after a person dies: we transfer all of the assets into the trust, so that *there is nothing for the probate court to do after a person dies*! The Ford Motor Company stock is transferred from "Fred Brown" (which would have necessitated a probate) to "Fred Brown, Trustee, The Fred Brown Family Trust." When Fred Brown dies, his *successor trustee* opens up the trust and reads it, and determines who gets what. The successor trustee does not need the assistance of the probate court to obtain title to the stock, the trust *already owns the stock*! You can wave at the probate court as you drive by, but you need not go inside.

We are sometimes asked if the probate court judges mind people using living trusts in order to avoid the probate court. They don't mind at all, to the same extent that criminal court judges don't mind if people don't commit crimes.

Remember that creating a living trust alone does not accomplish the probate avoidance. We need to transfer title of the probatable assets into the trust. We don't need to do anything with respect to the life insurance policies and the retirement plans, since they already escape probate. We invariably remind clients at the time we set up a living trust that they will likely acquire assets in the ensuing years, and that they must remember to title the newly-acquired assets in the name of the trust, not in their own names. If they forget, and one of them dies, the result will be a probate, just to get one or two assets into the hands of the intended beneficiaries.

After everything we've just said about how living trusts avoid probate and how having only a will does not, it might surprise you to learn that preparing and signing a trust does not obviate the need for a will. If there is a trust, the will becomes a backup, and comes into play when an asset, through inadvertence, has not been transferred into the trust. The will serves as a "pour-over" will instructing the probate court to transfer any and all assets into the trust. The pour-over will avoids the decedent dying intestate with respect to the asset, and assures the asset is eventually distributed in accordance with the decedent's desires. The pour-over will is a poor substitute for titling the asset in the name of the trust; a probate is necessary to get the asset into the trust.

California's "Small Estate" Procedure

The reason that we asked out caller about the amounts in dad's checking accounts was not because we're nosy, but because on the answer might depend on whether the estate needs to go through probate or not.

California has a procedure that permits the heirs of certain smaller estates to avoid probate. If, in the aggregate, the *probatable assets* do not exceed $150,000, then the heirs can present an affidavit to the persons holding the assets (banks, brokerage firms, etc), swearing that they are entitled to the assets and that the probatable assets do not exceed $150,000. For some reason, the law requires the heirs to wait at least 40 days from the date of the decedent's death before they may present the affidavit. In determining whether the estate qualifies, the heirs do not have to count any assets that don't go through probate, such as life insurance, retirement plan assets and property held in joint tenancy. Remember, you can use the Small Estate procedure only if the probatable assets, *in the aggregate*, do not exceed $150,000. On many occasions, heirs will go to one bank with an affidavit and clear an account that has $100,000 in it, and go to another bank with another affidavit and clear another $100,000 account. People do it, and it works, but it's not exactly legal.

A Few Words About Estate Taxes

The reason that we're going to devote only a few words to estate taxes is that most single people, and even fewer married couples, are not subject to federal estate taxes.

Here is most of what you need to know. If a person dies in 2015 with an estate whose assets are under $5,430,000, there are no estate taxes. The exemption rises every year based on a cost-of-living adjustment (the exemption was $5,340,000 in 2014). That also means that a married couple with estates of close to $11 million will not be subject to estate taxes. Also, if you give what you have to your spouse upon your death, there are no estate taxes when the first spouse dies, regardless of the size of the estate. If a person does not wish to leave all or part of his or her estate to a surviving spouse, there are ways to avoid the imposition of estate taxes on the first death, but you will need a fairly complicated trust to accomplish that. It was just this provision in the tax code that resulted in Edith Windsor – who was legally married to her same-sex partner in Canada – having to pay an estate tax because the tax code did not recognize her same-sex marriage. Now that same-sex marriage is legal in California, there is no doubt that California same-sex spouses who leave their estates to their surviving spouses will incur no estate taxes when the first spouse dies.

Advance Health Care Directives

We have all heard the horror stories of life partners who were denied access to their partners' sick beds and deathbeds because they were not married.

These stories are horrible, but they are also avoidable, even in those states that still refuse to recognize same-sex marriage.

California allows any adult to write an *Advance Health Care Directive*, (sometimes referred to as a "living will") which enables a person to appoint anyone else (not just a spouse) as his or her health care agent, empowered to make health care decisions for a person who is unable to make those decisions for himself or herself. One of the most important decisions that you can authorize your agent to make is the decision to refuse or terminate life support in the event you are comatose. A typical Advance Health Care Directive will provide:

"I do not want my life to be prolonged if (1) I have an incurable and
irreversible condition that will result in my death within a relatively
short time; (2) I become unconscious and, to a reasonable degree of
medical certainty, I will not regain consciousness, or (3) the likely risks
and burdens of treatment would outweigh the expected benefits."

You may also use an Advance Health Care Directive to authorize -- or refuse to authorize -- the donation of body parts following your death.

If you name your spouse as your health care agent, and your spouse predeceases you, you have lost your health care agent. You can name an alternate agent -- or agents -- to step in if your health care agent predeceases you or otherwise cannot or will not serve.

Federal law requires every hospital to ask you if you have an Advance Health Care Directive at the time of admission to the hospital. But there is no law that requires you to have one, and no hospital will assist you in making one. It's best to do it beforehand.

Index

About the Authors

Robert F. Klueger J.D., LL.M

Robert F. Klueger is a partner in the law firm Klueger & Stein, LLP in Encino California. A practicing attorney since 1974, he is a member of the bars of the United States Supreme Court, the United States Tax Court and the state bars of California, New York and Colorado.

He received his J.D. degree from Fordham Law School, New York, and a Master of Laws in Taxation from the University of Denver. He has been accredited by the State Bar of California as a Certified Tax Law Specialist.

This is Mr. Klueger's seventh published book. This is his first collaboration with Elizabeth Klueger, his daughter.

Elizabeth A. Klueger, Esq.

Elizabeth A. Klueger is a licensed attorney with experience in consumer protection law and children's rights law, but most of her experience and focus is on California Estate Planning. She is a passionate advocate and a legal voice for the young, emerging leaders of the LGBT community.

Ms. Klueger has a Juris Doctorate and is licensed to practice in the state of California. She earned her B.A. in Liberal Arts with a focus on Philosophy from The Evergreen State College in Olympia, WA. She received her law degree from Southwestern Law School in Los Angeles, California. This is her first published book.

Learn more and review updates at
www.kluegerestateplanning.com

ISBN:150786230X

www.ingramcontent.com/pod-product-compliance
Lightning Source LLC
Chambersburg PA
CBHW070837180526
45168CB00002B/861